VEGAN CAKES

dreamy cakes and decadent desserts

SARAH HARDY

photography by Stephanie McLeod

Hardie Grant

QUADRILLE

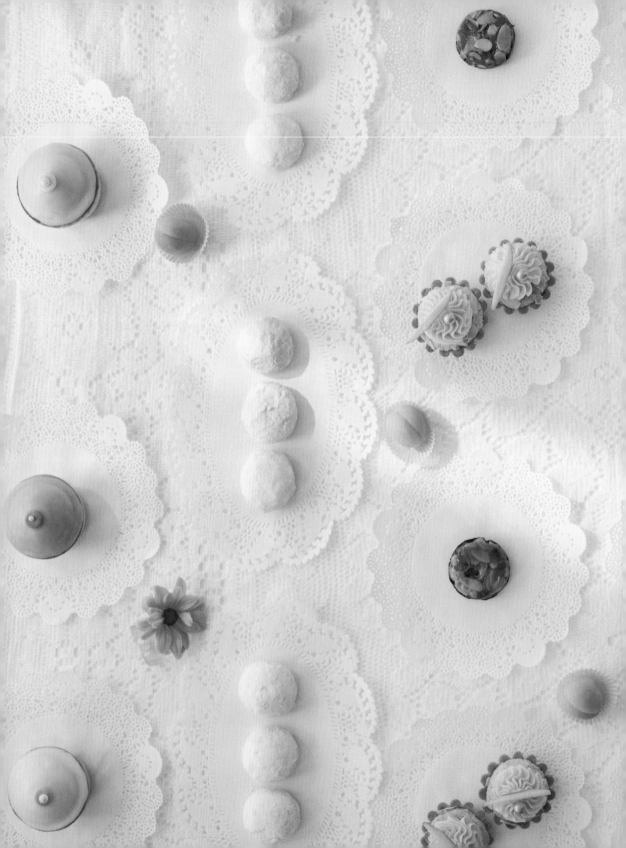

INTRODUCTION

Vegan cakes and desserts tend to get a bad rap. I've had my fair share of dry and bland vegan cakes, and many people who are new to the concept of vegan food still have the misconception that 'vegan' equals healthy. In this book I want to show you how vegan cakes and desserts can be just as indulgent and delicious as their dairy- and egg-laden counterparts, as well as being beautiful to look at.

As a self-taught baker most of my knowledge of baking has been acquired through experimentation and trial and error. There are always new ingredients and products that are being introduced to the market, which make vegan baking really exciting as it's constantly evolving. If you are new to vegan baking there may be ingredients in this book which you have not heard of before, that I will go into more depth about later on. With the recent growth of the vegan food trend it should be easy to find all ingredients used in this book at your local health food store or supermarket, as well as online.

This book contains many 'veganized' classics, as well as some more adventurous flavours and desserts you may not have tried before. I have also included step-by-step techniques and photo diagrams for all of the decorating methods used in this book, which should help you in creating your own dreamy cakes and decadent desserts. Share your creations with me on Instagram @hebe_konditori.

KITCHEN EQUIPMENT

The following is a list of some tools and pieces of equipment that you will need to make the recipes in the book. Some things aren't essential but will make the process much easier.

CAKE TINS

When making layered cakes it's best to use simple cake tins with straight edges and without loose bottoms or springform releases – this will ensure that your cake layers are as uniform as possible. Loose-bottomed tins are useful for things like cheesecakes or tarts that need to be carefully removed from the tin.

STAND MIXER

I specify using a stand mixer in recipes as they come with different attachments, making them very versatile. However, if you don't own one you can use an electric hand whisk for mixing cake batters. For doughs you'll need to knead by hand and add around 4 minutes to the time it needs to be worked.

RUBBER SPATULA

I always use one of these for stirring and folding by hand. They're really good for getting every last scrap of mix out of the bowl and they won't scratch your pans. Make sure you purchase a heat-safe one.

MEASURING SPOONS

These are very handy as many recipes in this book call for teaspoons and tablespoons and it can be quite tricky measuring out ingredients without them.

CAKE TURNTABLE

This makes assembling layer cakes and covering cakes with buttercream much easier. I'd recommend a metal one as they're much sturdier and last a lot longer than plastic turntables. However, they are much more expensive so if you're not planning to make a lot of layer cakes then a plastic one will do just fine too.

CAKE SCRAPER

I like using a metal cake scraper as I find they get a really sharp buttercream edge on your cake, but plastic versions are available too. They are also great for cleaning your work surface after you've been working with dough or anything sticky.

SMALL OFFSET SPATULA

Useful for smoothing out buttercream on cakes and smoothing the top of cake batters before they go into the oven.

FONDANT SMOOTHER

This is literally just a piece of flat plastic with a handle on the back – but it's very handy for smoothing fondant and marzipan coverings.

PARCHMENT PAPER

It's really important to use non-stick parchment paper and not greaseproof baking paper as most of your bakes will end up getting totally stuck if you use the latter. You can also use silicone mats but the good-quality ones are quite expensive.

FOOD PROCESSOR

You will need one of these for quite a few recipes in the book. If you don't have one you could use a blender like Nutribullet – you'll just have to blitz things in batches.

SMALL BLENDER

This is just a smaller version of a food processor but it's useful for blending small quantities of nuts, like when making whipped cashew cream (see page 146). It will allow you to get super-smooth nut butters and creams, as well as smooth fruit purées.

ROLLING PIN

For rolling pastry, fondant and marzipan you'll need a 20cm (8in) rolling pin without a handle – a solid shape is ideal so that you never have to worry about making marks on your pastry or fondant.

DISPOSABLE PIPING BAGS

Readily available online and in cake decorating shops, these are pretty essential for decorating. They come in a lot of sizes but I tend to use small 15cm (6in) bags for royal icing and small detail piping, and larger bags of about 30cm (12in) for filling and covering layer cakes. You can also purchase reusable piping bags; however, I find it trickier to source nozzles to fit them. If using disposable piping bags, make sure they are biodegradable.

NOZZLES

These come in all shapes and sizes. I always use metal nozzles as the plastic ones don't tend to create as defined shapes. To use, simply cut a small hole at the bottom of the piping bag, just big enough for the tip to come through. See pages 20–23 for some basic piping techniques using nozzles.

SUGAR THERMOMETER

Vital for Italian meringue buttercream and a few other recipes. You can use the water test instead but it isn't always completely accurate. To do this, use a clean spoon to drop a little sugar syrup into a bowl of very cold water then remove from the water immediately. If it is sticky and malleable it has reached the soft ball stage. If it holds together in a ball it is at hard ball stage and perfect for making the Italian merigue buttercream on page 143. If it hardens as soon as it hits the water and snaps under pressure then it is perfect for the lollipops on page 136.

OVEN TEMPS

The oven temperatures given are for standard ovens. If your oven is fan-assisted (convection) please lower the temperature by 10–20°C/ 20–30°F.

BASIC
INGREDIENTS

Below are some basic ingredients that are my staples of vegan baking. If you're new to vegan cooking there may be some ingredients you're not familiar with yet.

SOAKED CASHEW NUTS

Soaking cashews lets them absorb water and become much softer. This makes them much easier to blend and turn into creamy textures. They also have a fairly neutral flavour, which makes them a great base for lots of recipes. To soak cashews simply place in a bowl and cover with cold water, then leave at room temperature for about 3 hours. You can also leave them overnight, but make sure you cover the bowl and place it in the fridge.

COCONUT OIL

Recipes will specify refined or unrefined coconut oil. Unlike unrefined coconut oil, the refined oil doesn't have a coconut flavour. It also has a higher smoking point, which makes it more suitable for baking and heating. Note that it is solid at room temperature so occasionally you will need to melt it before being able to use it.

UNSWEETENED MILK & YOGURT ALTERNATIVES

With any of the recipes that call for vegan milk or yogurt in this book, it's important to use ones that are unsweetened and unflavoured, as added sweeteners and ingredients could affect the bake or finished outcome of your cakes and desserts. There are lots of dairy-free alternatives available now so use whichever one you prefer – I tend to use oat milk for all my bakes but I will specify in the recipe when to use a particular dairy-free alternative if necessary.

BAKING BLOCK

For all the recipes in the book that require vegan butter I use Naturli baking block as it bakes and melts much more like regular butter. It's made from a mix of shea butter oil, coconut oil and rapeseed oil, which makes it much firmer than other vegan spreads and so is perfect for buttercream.

POTATO PROTEIN

I'm not sure about you, but I just can't stomach the taste of aquafaba. I've tried using beans other than chickpeas but the smell of the stuff alone just doesn't seem right. Potato protein, however, is like magic dust! It has no flavour, creates amazing firm peaks when making meringue and in terms of cost per use is cheaper than both eggs and aquafaba. It's available to buy online (see stockists on page 155).

POTATO STARCH

Not to be confused with potato flour, potato starch is a fine white powder, somewhat similar to cornflour (cornstarch) but I find it has a more neutral taste. When added to plain (all-purpose) flour in a cake it produces a lighter sponge. You will find it in most heath food stores or online.

PSYLLIUM HUSK

This is an all-natural fibre that, when mixed with water, swells to 10 times its original size. It's also colourless and flavourless and is used for binding and thickening in baked goods to make a more tender crumb.

XANTHAN GUM

This is a thickener and stabilizer that is produced from fermented glucose or sucrose. It's most commonly seen in gluten-free baking but works well as a thickener in vegan cooking too.

COCONUT CREAM

You will see this quite a bit in the book. To make, simply place a can of coconut milk in the fridge overnight, then open the can and scoop out the solid white bit from the top. Whip it up using a whisk and you have coconut cream. You can buy this ready-made but it's not as easy to come by.

APPLE SAUCE

You can by this ready-made – just make sure it's unsweetened – but I have included a recipe in the book (see page 149). I use it in sponges to make them super-moist and fluffy.

AGAR AGAR POWDER

This vegan gelatin substitute is extracted from red algae and is pretty easy to find in most supermarkets. It doesn't have quite the same texture as gelatin but it's flavourless and allows you to set your jellies at room temperature.

FOOD COLOURINGS

I only use gel food colouring for my recipes. They're much more concentrated than liquid food colourings and are essential for colouring things like fondant or marzipan, as liquid colouring adds too much moisture and you'll end up with a sticky mess. They're easy to find in most cake decorating shops and online. I use Sugarflair gels as they are certified vegan.

GRAPESEED OIL

I like to use grapeseed oil in my bakes as it has a very neutral flavour but, if you can't get hold of it, simply use sunflower or vegetable oil instead.

VEGAN EVERYTHING

It's always important to check your products are fully vegan as some companies use non-vegan products or processes to make the final product. I also steer away from using products that contain palm oil and try to ensure that everything I use is ethically sourced.

BASIC TECHNIQUES

LAYERING CAKES

Here are some key things to learn when it comes to making layer cakes. A lot of what I know has come through trial and error, so here are my top tips for making sure you avoid any disasters when assembling your cakes.

Level your cake

When creating a layer cake your starting point has to be sponges with flat, level tops. If your sponges have domed tops or an uneven surface and you fill your layers with buttercream then chances are a lot of the filling is going to ooze out of the edges. Uneven layers also mean that the weight distribution is not even and when the sponges are stacked this can lead to splitting. Levelling works well on any sponge that doesn't have too many whole ingredients (the fruits and nuts in things like carrot cake or fruit cake will drag the knife and you'll end up with a very crumby cake top).

You will need:

cake turntable

large serrated knife

1 Place your first sponge layer on the cake turntable. I like to do this as it brings the sponge closer to eye level, and makes it easy to rotate while you cut.

2 Work out where the doming begins, hold one hand over the top of the sponge and, with the other, hold your knife as level as possible against the side of the cake and carefully start to cut using a gentle sawing motion. Make sure you go slowly and try not to drag the knife though the sponge as you'll end up with a wonky cut. Continue until you have reached the other side. Repeat with your remaining sponges. (This is also the perfect opportunity to try some cake scraps before the finished thing.)

Filling your cake

The next step to consider when making your layer cake is the filling. The main thing you'll need to watch out for here is overfilling and using fillings that are too soft or runny (although damming can help here, see page 16). I prefer to pipe my filling rather than spoon it on as it makes it much easier to maintain an even layer.

You will need:

cake board that is 2.5cm (1in) larger than your cake

cake turntable

piping bag

offset spatula

scissors

CONTINUED OVERLEAF...

1 Place a cake board on your turntable and put a small blob of buttercream in the centre before placing a sponge layer on top, cut side up.

2 Put the buttercream or filling into a piping bag. Cut a hole at the bottom about 1cm (½in) wide and then, starting from the middle, pipe a swirl of the buttercream onto the cake, covering around 40–50 per cent of the surface.

3 Then take your offset spatula and smooth the buttercream into an even layer, going right to the edges of the sponge and filling all the gaps (I spin the turntable while I do this to make it quicker).

4 If this is all the filling you're adding then add the next layer of sponge cut side up, pressing down slightly, and repeat until you reach the top layer. Place the last sponge cut side down (this will make it easier to crumb coat).

Damming

This technique is used to stop any soft or runny fillings oozing out of the cake, such as compote or caramel. These fillings normally sit on top of the first layer of buttercream. Regular buttercream is normally used to make the dam but sometimes, if you're working with a heavier cake, you would add more icing sugar to the buttercream to stiffen it up and make it sturdier. (In this book you will only ever need to use the buttercream already stated in the recipe to make your dam.)

1 With your buttercream layer complete (see step 2 of 'Filling your cake'), pipe a line of buttercream all the way around the edge of the buttercream layer, then fill with the compote or caramel. Make sure the compote or caramel doesn't come up higher that the buttercream dam, as it will spill out of the sides of the cake. Continue stacking your sponges, damming between each layer, until you reach the top. Place the final layer cut side down.

Crumb coating

Now that your cake is fully stacked, you need to crumb coat. Crumb coating is done to create an even layer for the final buttercream coating to stick to and to trap any loose crumbs that you don't want showing up on the finished cake.

You will need:

cake turntable

small offset spatula

cake scraper

1 Using your piping bag of buttercream, pipe buttercream onto the sides of the cake in a zigzag motion from top to bottom. Work all the way around the sides, covering about 30–40 per cent of the cake. Then pipe a swirl of buttercream on top of the cake; you only need to cover about 30 per cent of the top. At this stage you are simply coating the cake with a very thin layer of buttercream.

2 Use an offset spatula to spread the buttercream until it is as smooth as you can get on both the top and sides. Then take your cake scraper and smooth off any excess buttercream until you have an even layer all over the cake. If there are any gaps go back around, filling in with the excess buttercream and smoothing out once more (see page 18 for further step photos).

3 Place your cake in the fridge for at least 3 hours (or as stated in the recipe) for the cake and buttercream to firm up. This will also make it a lot easier to apply the final layer of buttercream.

Final coating

This is where it gets a bit trickier. I used to be hopeless at doing this, but a lot of that was down to me using buttercream that was too stiff and not giving my cake enough time in the fridge before the final coating. One thing that makes this step a lot easier is using Italian meringue buttercream as it doesn't form a crust like American-style buttercream does. You can still get a great finish on your American buttercream cakes; you just need to be a bit quicker when icing so that it doesn't harden before you're finished.

You will need:

cake turntable

small offset spatula

cake scraper

1 This is pretty much the same technique as crumb coating but you want to apply your buttercream much more thickly this time. Begin by piping a spiral of buttercream on top of the cake, making sure to go right to the edges, covering about 50–60 per cent of the top. Pipe around the sides in a zigzag motion as before, starting from the very bottom edge going all the way up to the top edge. Again you want to cover about 50–60 per cent of the cake.

2 Next you want to go in with your offset spatula. Starting with the top of the cake, hold your offset spatula flat against the buttercream and smooth out, spinning the turntable as you do. You want to have a smooth layer of buttercream that spills over the edges of the cake. Then smooth out the sides of the cake, filling in all the gaps.

3 When you've got your buttercream as smooth as possible with the offset spatula, swap to your cake scraper. Starting with the top of your cake, hold the scraper flat against the middle of the cake and spin the turntable to smooth. Then move to the sides of the cake. Hold the scraper parallel to the side of the cake and make sure that the bottom edge is flush with the cake board then pull the scraper along while turning the turntable. Continue until the icing is as smooth as possible.

4 When both the sides and top are smooth you'll probably have a bit of a messy top edge where the buttercream has been pushed up from the scraper. Using an offset spatula, drag the buttercream into the centre of the cake to create a sharp edge.

5 Go over the top of your cake once more with the scraper and your cake is finished.

PIPING BUTTERCREAM

I use a few different piping techniques in this book and all are really easy to master with a little practice. I'd recommend practising on some parchment paper before going straight onto your cake if you've never tried piping before.

TRAILING SHELL BORDER

Fill a piping bag fitted with a star or French star tip with buttercream. Holding the piping bag at a 45-degree angle, pipe on blobs of buttercream; as you release the pressure swipe down to taper the shell. Start the next shell on the trail of the one before.

WIGGLES

Fill a piping bag fitted with a petal tip with buttercream. Pipe with the narrow edge facing upwards, then wiggle the piping bag left to right as you pull backwards.

RUFFLE BORDER

Fill a piping bag fitted with a petal tip with buttercream. Pipe with the wider end touching the cake and wiggle the piping bag slightly as you pull backwards.

RUFFLES

Fill a piping bag fitted with a closed star tip or French star tip with buttercream. If using the closed star tip, pipe three concentric swirls, flicking up at the end. For the French star tip, bob the bag up and down as you pipe, then flick up at the end.

SCALLOP BORDER

Fill a piping bag fitted with a round tip with buttercream. This is pretty much the same as the shell technique. Hold the bag at a 45-degree angle from the cake, pipe a blob of buttercream and then swipe down. Start the next scallop where the previous one finishes.

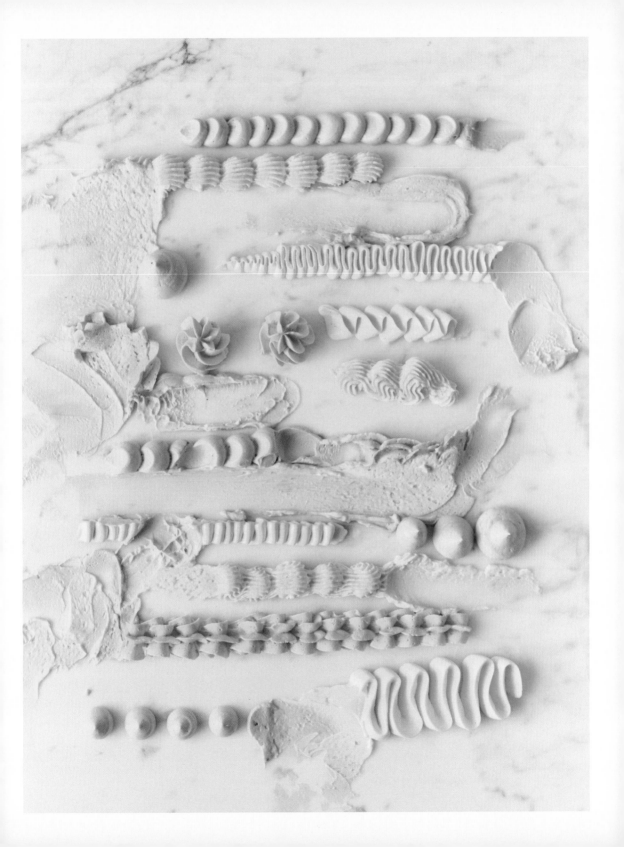

PIPING ROYAL ICING

Below is my recipe for a basic royal icing. I use quite a loose mixture compared to some, as I find it easier to use and quicker to pipe with. I'd recommend practising on parchment paper or a work surface before going straight to your cake.

250g (9oz) icing (confectioners') sugar

1 tsp cornflour (cornstarch)

¼ tsp xanthan gum

3 tbsp water (you may need more or less)

food colouring (optional)

1 Sift your dry ingredients into a bowl and mix until evenly combined, then gradually add the water a tablespoon at a time, mixing with each addition (you may not need all of it).

2 To test the icing is the right consistency, pull up a spoonful of icing and then let a thin trail of the mixture drop back into the bowl. It should be able to hold its folds when dropped without dissolving back into the rest of the mixture.

Swags / string work

These are what I use on the pink vanilla dream cake (see page 30) and are most often seen on classic Marie Antoinette-style cakes. These will take a bit of practice but once you've cracked it you'll be doing them on all your cakes.

You will need:

parchment paper

scissors

no. 2 or 1.5 round nozzle

small piping bag

1 To mark out where your swags are going to go, cut out a circle of paper that's just a bit smaller than the top of the cake. Fold this in half three times, then unfold, so that you have eight segments. Place the piece of paper on top of the cake and use the fold marks to lightly mark out even points around the top edge of the cake with a toothpick or knife.

2 Once you have your marks, fit the piping bag with the nozzle and fill with your royal icing, pushing down so it's all at the very bottom/nozzle end. With your non-dominant hand, hold the top of the piping bag to stop any icing falling out and, with your other hand, hold and squeeze the piping bag about 5cm (2in) away from the top of the piping nozzle.

3 Hold the piping bag so it's about a 45-degree angle from the side of the cake and the tip is about a millimetre away from one of your marks. Apply pressure until the icing adheres to the cake then, using the same amount of pressure, pull the tip away and across to make a string of icing. You want to let it hang a little to create the swooping swag shape, then touch the tip back to the next mark to finish the swag.

4 To pipe layers of multiple swags, I find it easiest to start with the smallest. I do each one around the cake and then move on to the slightly larger swag below and then finish with the largest one below that. To make your swags bigger simply let your line of icing hang for slightly longer.

Writing

With writing I find it much easier to use cursive writing as you don't have to keep stopping and starting, but some people find writing individual letters easier as you have more control. Here I will explain how to write using both techniques. The method is somewhat similar to the swags (see page 22) in that we want to create a piece of string with the icing rather than piping as if you're using a pen (which results in squiggly lines and much less control of the lettering).

You will need:

no. 1.5 or 2 round nozzle (but you can use a larger nozzle if you prefer)

small piping bag

1 Fit your piping bag with the nozzle and then fill with your royal icing, pushing down so all the icing is at the tip. With your non-dominant hand, hold the bag at the top, to stop any icing falling out and then, with your other hand, hold close to the tip around 5cm (2in) away from the nozzle.

2 To pipe separate letters, apply pressure at the start of the line, touching the icing to the cake so it adheres. Lift up and away to create a string of icing and then release the pressure just before the end point so you don't end up with a blob of icing when you touch back down. To ensure all of your letters end up the same size and in a straight line, use each letter as a guide for the next.

3 For cursive lettering you use the same sort of technique but hold the piping tip closer to the cake and drag your lines along to join up the letters. You will still need to stop and start occasionally with this technique, but on the whole it's much quicker than doing every letter separately.

4 If you make any small mistakes as you go then you can use a small, damp paintbrush to nudge the lines slightly. If you make any larger mistakes, I find it best to wait for the icing to dry completely, pick off the lettering using the tip of a knife or small palette knife and then start over.

Sprinkles

Royal icing is also great for making sprinkles in whatever design you like. Pipe your designs onto a sheet of parchment paper and then leave to dry out completely for around 12 hours, depending on the size. When dry, tip your sprinkles into an airtight container and store until you need them.

FONDANT & MARZIPAN COVERING

Fondant and marzipan covering definitely divides people on taste – you either love the stuff or hate it. Either way it makes your cakes look extra polished and you'll be impressing everyone with your decorating skills. You'll need a crumb-coated and fully chilled cake before you begin. I leave mine in the fridge for around 6 hours or overnight to make sure the cake is sturdy enough. Ensure you place your cake on a cake board before you start as this will make it much easier to manoeuvre. Marzipan and fondant can both easily be bought at your local supermarket, but do ensure that they're vegan. For homemade marzipan follow the recipe on page 140.

You will need:

a fully chilled and crumb coated cake

cornflour (cornstarch), for dusting

about 1kg (2¼lb) marzipan or fondant (or both)

large rolling pin

cake turntable or cake stand

fondant smoother

sharp knife

1 Start by measuring your cake so you know how much marzipan/fondant you'll need to cover the whole thing. I use the rolling pin to roughly do this – measure up one side of the cake, across the top and then back down the other side. This will give you the diameter you'll need, but add a few centimetres (an inch) for good measure. For a three-layer 20cm (8in) cake you'll need about 1kg (2¼lb) marzipan/fondant.

2 Lightly dust a large smooth surface with a little cornflour and knead your marzipan/fondant for a couple of minutes to soften it up. If you're adding colour, do this now. Continue kneading until soft, malleable and your colour (if using) is evenly combined.

3 Dust your surface with cornflour again, if needed, and then begin to roll out the marzipan/fondant. You want to make sure to turn it frequently to achieve an even thickness and ensure it rolls into a circular shape.

4 When you have rolled out the marzipan/fondant to the correct diameter, and it's an even thickness of about 3mm (⅛in), you're ready to transfer it to your cake. If you've rolled it out too big, simply cut the excess off with a knife.

5 Position the cake on the work surface. Pick the marzipan/fondant up by flipping one half over the rolling pin. Drape one side of the over the cake (I usually start from the back side) and roll the rolling pin out from underneath as you cover the whole of the cake.

CONTINUED OVERLEAF...

6 Using your hands, you want to start sticking the marzipan/fondant to the cake around the top edge; this will ensure there's no tearing from the weight of the marzipan/fondant pulling down. Then start pulling out and down, very gently, around the bottom edge of the cake to remove any ripples. Once you have done this, transfer your cake to a cake turntable or cake stand and start using the fondant smoother. Use a circular and up and down rubbing motion to smooth out any little wrinkles that need fixing.

7 When your cake is looking smooth, you then want to seal the bottom edge. Use the fondant smoother to press down on the marzipan/fondant at the base of the cake. Go round the cake a couple of times until it looks totally sealed. Then use a knife to cut away the excess fondant.

8 Finally, go back round with your fondant smoothers and give it one last smooth out. Your layer cake is now ready for decoration.

DREAMY

CAKES

PINK VANILLA DREAM CAKE

This cake really is a dream! Super-fluffy vanilla sponge sandwiched together with tart rhubarb compote and silky pink buttercream and then decorated with pink swags and buttercream shells. A cake fit for Marie Antoinette herself!

FOR THE CAKE

300g (1½ cups) caster (superfine) sugar

350g (2½ cups) self-raising flour

50g (½ cup) cornflour (cornstarch)

½ tsp fine sea salt

1 tbsp baking powder

200g (7oz) vegan butter (at room temperature), cubed, plus extra for greasing

190g (6¾oz) unsweetened vegan yogurt

200ml (¾ cup) dairy-free milk

1 tbsp vanilla extract

few drops of pink food colouring

TO ASSEMBLE

1 batch of Italian meringue buttercream (see page 143)

pink food colouring

250g (9oz) rhubarb compote (see page 150 for homemade)

800g–1kg (1¾–2¼lb) pale pink fondant

100g (3½oz) pink royal icing (see page 22)

dragees (optional)

1 Preheat the oven to 190°C/375°F/Gas 5 and grease and line the base of three 20cm (8in) cake tins with parchment paper.

2 Sift all the dry ingredients into the bowl of your stand mixer and mix gently to combine. Add the cubed butter to the bowl, then fit the paddle attachment to the mixer (or use an electric hand whisk) and beat together on a low speed until the mixture resembles fine breadcrumbs.

3 In a separate bowl whisk together the yogurt, milk, vanilla and two drops of pink food colouring. Pour into the bowl of the mixer and beat on low until fully combined. Scrape down the sides of the bowl then increase the speed to medium-high and beat for about 2 minutes until the mixture is light and fluffy.

4 Pour the batter evenly into the three cake tins, then smooth out the tops using an offset spatula. Bake in the oven for 20–25 minutes; when baked the sponges will spring back when lightly pressed. Leave in the tins for about 10 minutes before turning out onto a wire rack to cool fully. Once fully cooled, use a large serrated knife to slice off the rounded dome tops so you have a level surface for stacking (see page 15).

5 Meanwhile, make the Italian meringue buttercream according to the instructions on page 143 then add a few drops of pink food colouring until you have your desired shade of pink. Transfer about two-thirds of the buttercream to a piping bag and cut a 1cm (½ in) hole in the end.

CONTINUED OVERLEAF...

6 Place one of the sponges on a cake board using a blob of buttercream to secure it. Then pipe a layer of buttercream onto the sponge and smooth with an offset spatula. Pipe a buttercream dam around the edge (see page 16), then fill with half of the rhubarb compote before topping with the next layer of sponge. Repeat to make the second layer, then place the third layer of cake on the top, cut side down. Crumb coat the whole cake and refrigerate for at least 3 hours. (See pages 15–19 for more detailed instructions.)

7 When the cake is chilled, roll out your fondant and follow the instructions on pages 25–27 to cover your cake. Make the royal icing accoring to the instructions on page 22 and transfer to a small piping bag. Write a message on your cake, if you like, and then pipe swags around the top edge of the cake (see page 22).

8 Put the remaining buttercream into a piping bag fitted with a small/medium French star nozzle. Pipe one large shell between each swag by holding the piping bag at a 45-degree angle from the side of the cake. Hovering the tip over where you want the shell to start, squeeze the bag while pulling up and releasing the pressure so that the shell tapers at the top. Use the same technique to pipe a border around the top and bottom of the cake (see page 20).

9 You can finish the cake by gently pressing dragees into the fondant at the tops of the shells and between the swags.

BANANA MALTED MILK ROLL

Avoid using overly ripe bananas when making the sponge for this cake as the sugars in the bananas will give the cake a much darker colour and you will lose all definition in your stripes.

FOR THE CAKE

150g (1¼ cups) plain (all-purpose) flour

¾ tsp bicarbonate of soda (baking soda)

½ tsp salt

160g (5½oz) bananas (about 1½ large bananas)

50g (¼ cup) caster (superfine) sugar

50g (¼ cup) soft light brown sugar

70g (2½oz) vegan butter, plus extra for greasing

3 tbsp oat milk

¾ tsp apple cider vinegar

1 tsp vanilla extract

2 drops of yellow food colouring

FOR THE BANANA JAM

150g (5oz) very ripe bananas

60g (2¼oz) caster (superfine) sugar

1 tbsp lemon juice

⅛ tsp fine sea salt

1 Preheat the oven to 180°C/350°F/Gas 4. Grease a shallow baking tin 20 x 30cm (8 x 12in) and line the base and sides with parchment paper, making sure the paper overhangs the tray so it's easy to remove the sponge after baking.

2 To make the banana jam, mash the bananas until quite smooth. Then add to a small pan along with the rest of the ingredients. Cook over a medium heat for about 10 minutes, stirring frequently with a whisk, until the jam reaches the consistency of a thick caramel sauce. Remove from the heat and set aside to cool while you make the cake.

3 Sift together the flour, bicarbonate of soda and salt in a bowl then set aside. In a food processor, blitz the bananas until smooth (or mash using a fork), then place in a large bowl with all the remaining ingredients, except the yellow food colouring. Beat together, then add the dry ingredients and mix again until combined.

4 Transfer half of the cake batter to a large piping bag. Add the food colouring to the remaining batter in the bowl, mix and then add to another piping bag. Snip the tips off the bags and pipe alternate stripes of batter diagonally across the baking sheet. Bake in the oven for 10–12 minutes.

5 When the cake is baked (it should feel lightly springy to the touch), you need to pre-roll it while it's still hot. Run a knife around the edge of the tin and then, using the parchment paper as handles, pull out the cake onto a worktop. Lightly dust the surface of the cake with icing sugar, then cover with another sheet of parchment paper. Starting from a short end, begin rolling the sponge into a swiss roll shape, trying to do so as tightly as possible. Leave to cool completely.

CONTINUED OVERLEAF...

FOR THE MALTED MILK BUTTERCREAM

110g (4oz) vegan butter

100g (3½oz) icing (confectioners') sugar, plus extra for dusting

40g (1½oz) malt extract

1 drop of yellow food colouring

6 To make the buttercream, put all the ingredients into the bowl of a stand mixer fitted with the paddle attachment (or use an electric hand whisk) and then beat together, occasionally scraping down the sides of the bowl, until the buttercream is light and fluffy.

7 When your rolled sponge is cool to the touch you need to carfeully unroll it and gently peel off the parchment paper. Lay the sponge on a fresh piece of parchment paper ready to roll up again.

8 To assemble the cake, spread an even layer of banana jam over the surface of the sponge, leaving 5cm (2in) uncovered at one short end. Then spread a layer of the malt buttercream over the top of the jam, again leaving a gap at the end. Starting at the fully iced, short end of the cake, begin rolling, use the parchment paper to help you roll the cake. The first bit will be the most difficult so go slowly. Keep rolling, trying to roll as tightly as possible.

9 When the cake is fully rolled, place it on a sheet of clingfilm (plastic wrap) and roll it up tightly, then seal the ends. Place in the fridge for at least 1 hour. When the cake has chilled remove the clingfilm and then trim both ends of the cake. Serve in generous slices.

24 CARROT GOLD CAKE

My favourite version of this cake used to be the one from Costco. But it must be said I do have a love of refined sugar (the Fondant Fancy is, in my opinion, potentially the greatest cake ever created – I'm still working on a vegan recipe for those). This cake is packed with spice, pecans and sultanas and slathered in an orange zest cream cheese buttercream. The inspiration for this cake came from 'The Golden Age' of Greek mythology, hence the Grecian pillars.

FOR THE CAKE
vegan butter, for greasing

300g (2¼ cups) plain (all-purpose) flour

175g (generous ¾ cup) soft light brown sugar

175g (generous ¾ cup) caster (superfine) sugar

2 tsp baking powder

1 tsp bicarbonate of soda (baking soda)

2 tsp ground cinnamon

1 tsp ginger

½ tsp grated nutmeg

1 tsp fine sea salt

110ml (½ cup) grapeseed oil

230g (8oz) apple sauce (see page 149 for homemade)

180ml (¾ cup) dairy-free milk

75g (2½oz) sultanas (golden raisins)

3 tbsp rum

150g (5oz) grated yellow carrots (orange carrots are also fine)

50g (1¾oz) chopped pecans

FOR THE CREAM CHEESE FROSTING
250g (9oz) vegan cream cheese

175g (6oz) vegan butter (softened)

zest of 2 oranges

¼ tsp fine sea salt

450g (1lb) icing (confectioners') sugar

2 drops of peach food colouring

TO ASSEMBLE
1 batch of meringue pillars, about 13cm (5in) high (see page 134)

few sheets of edible gold leaf (optional)

1 Grease and line three 15cm (6in) cake tins and preheat the oven to 180°C/350°F/Gas 4.

2 Sift all of the dry ingredients into a large bowl. Put the oil, apple sauce and milk into a separate bowl and mix together.

3 Put the sultanas in a small bowl along with the rum and heat in the microwave for 1–2 minutes, or in a small pan, until the sultanas are plump.

4 Add the oil, apple and milk mixture to the dry ingredients and stir to combine, then add the sultanas, carrots and pecans. Mix until everything is evenly combined.

5 Pour the cake batter evenly into the three prepared cake tins and bake for 35–40 minutes. Leave to cool in the tins for 10 minutes before transferring to a wire rack to cool completely. Once fully cooled, use a large serrated knife to slice off the rounded dome tops so you have a level surface for stacking (see page 15).

6 To make the cream cheese frosting, place the cream cheese, softened butter, orange zest and salt in the bowl of a stand mixer fitted with the paddle attachment (or use an electric hand whisk). Beat together until smooth, scraping down the sides of the bowl occasionally to ensure everything is fully combined.

7 Add the icing sugar a little at a time and beat until smooth (make sure you cover the bowl with a cloth each time you mix to stop the sugar billowing out). Add the food colouring and mix again. Chill in the fridge for at least 1 hour before you begin frosting the cake.

8 Place a sponge layer on a cake stand or board, add a generous amount of buttercream and smooth out. Repeat with the other layers – you'll need to chill the cake between adding each layer to allow the buttercream to firm up as it is quite loose. Add a layer of crumb coating (see page 16) and place the cake in the fridge for at least 3 hours.

9 After chilling, apply a second layer of buttercream and smooth out with a cake scraper. Gently press the meringue pillars around the sides of the cake and, if you like, finish by gently pressing flecks of gold leaf onto the buttercream.

CHERRY BOMBE PRINCESS

Swedish princess cakes are usually made up of cake layers filled with crème patissière and raspberry compote, then topped with whipped cream. In this one, however, I use cherry pie filling and whipped cream between the layers. This cake is best made fresh on the day of eating.

FOR THE CAKE

150g (¾ cup) caster (superfine) sugar

175g (1¼ cups) self-raising flour

25g (¾oz) cornflour (cornstarch)

¼ tsp fine sea salt

½ tsp baking powder

100g (3½oz) vegan butter (at room temperature), cubed, plus extra for greasing

95g (3oz) unsweetened vegan yogurt

100ml (scant ½ cup) dairy-free milk

1½ tsp vanilla extract

few drops of pink food colouring

1 batch of cherry pie filling (see page 149)

FOR THE CREAM

1 batch of whipped cashew cream (see page 146)

100g (3½oz) icing (confectioners') sugar

1 Preheat the oven to 190°C/375°F/Gas 5 and grease and line the base of two 18cm (7in) cake tins with parchment paper.

2 Sift all the dry ingredients into the bowl of a stand mixer and whisk together (or use an electric hand whisk). Add the cubed butter to the dry ingredients, fit the mixer with the paddle attachment and beat together on a low speed until the mixture forms a fine breadcrumb texture.

3 Whisk the yogurt, milk, vanilla and pink food colouring together in a separate bowl. Add this to the cake mix and beat on low until combined. Scrape down the sides of the bowl then increase the speed to medium-high and beat together for approximately 2 minutes until the mixture is light and fluffy.

4 Divide the batter equally between the cake tins. Smooth out the top using an offset spatula and bake in the oven for 20–25 minutes. When baked the sponge will spring back when lightly pressed. Leave in the tins for about 10 minutes before turning out onto a wire rack to cool fully.

5 While the sponges are cooling, whip the cashew cream and icing sugar together in the bowl of a stand mixer (or use an electric hand whisk) until light and fluffy. Transfer two-thirds to a piping bag with a 1cm hole cut at the end (keep the rest for decoration).

CONTINUED ON PAGE 42...

TO DECORATE

cornflour (cornstarch), for dusting

300g (10½oz) marzipan (see page 140 for homemade)

few drops of pink food colouring

1 marzipan rose (see page 141)

2 marzipan leaves (see page 141)

white lustre spray

dragees

6 Once the sponges are fully cooled, use a large serrated knife to slice off the rounded dome tops so you have a level surface for stacking (see page 15). Now begin assembling. Stick the first sponge layer onto a cake board or serving plate using a blob of cream then pipe out a layer of cream over the cake (you don't want this too thick). Smooth out the cream using an offset spatula then pipe a dam around the edge of the cake (see page 16) and fill with the cherry pie filling. Top with the second sponge layer and then place in the fridge for about 30 minutes to 1 hour to firm up slightly.

7 When the cake is chilled, pipe a thin layer of cream over the sides of the cake and then add the rest of the cream to the top. Use an offset spatula to smooth out the sides, then smooth the cream on top of the cake into a dome shape. Take your time – you want a neat surface in preparation for the marzipan. Return the cake to the fridge for 30 minutes.

8 Lightly dust a work surface with cornflour and begin kneading the marzipan; add the pink colouring and continue kneading until the colour is even. Lightly dust your surface once more then roll out the marzipan, making sure you turn it frequently so you have an even, round layer that is a couple of millimetres (⅛in) thick.

9 Remove the cake from the fridge. Flip one half of the marzipan over your rolling pin and then drape over the cake, lifting the rolling pin out from underneath as you do so. Use your hands to gently smooth out the marzipan, removing any ripples by pulling the marzipan out and down. Then use a fondant smoother to smooth out any remaining wrinkles. Trim off the excess marzipan with a knife.

10 Add two-thirds of the reserved cream to a piping bag fitted with a large French star nozzle. Add the remaining third to another piping bag fitted with a small star nozzle or a Wilton 87 nozzle. Using the large nozzle, and starting at the centre of the cake, pipe 5 or 6 petal shapes to make a flower. Using the small nozzle, pipe dotted swags around the sides of the cake (or any pattern you'd prefer) and finish by piping a shell border around the bottom of the cake.

11 Top your cake with the marzipan rose and some marzipan leaves. Dot the swags with some dragees and spritz the whole thing with white lustre spray to finish.

BLACK TERRAZZO CHOCOLATE CAKE

Chocolate cake isn't actually one of my favourites, but I know it is for a lot of people and I always get asked to make them. So here is a recipe for a great chocolate cake: super-dark chocolate sponge filled with milk chocolate buttercream and covered in smooth vanilla, chocolate-bespeckled Italian meringue buttercream.

FOR THE CHOCOLATE CAKE

230g (8oz) plain (all-purpose) flour

1½ tsp bicarbonate of soda (baking soda)

½ tsp fine sea salt

80g (2¾oz) dark cocoa powder

150g (¾ cup) caster (superfine) sugar

150g (¾ cup) soft light brown sugar

360ml (1½ cups) soya milk

80g (2¾oz) vegan butter, plus extra for greasing

1½ tsp apple cider vinegar

½ tsp vanilla extract

60g (2¼oz) vegan dark chocolate

1 batch of Italian meringue buttercream (see page 143)

TO DECORATE

50g (1¾oz) vegan dark chocolate

15g (½oz) vegan butter

a few maraschino cherries (with stems)

1 Preheat the oven to 180°C/350°F/Gas 4 and grease and line the bases of three 15cm (6in) cake tins with parchment paper.

2 Sift together the flour, bicarbonate of soda, salt and cocoa powder into the bowl of a stand mixer fitted with the paddle attachment (or a large bowl).

3 Put both sugars, the soya milk and butter into a pan and heat gently until the sugars have fully dissolved. Remove from the heat then add the cider vinegar and vanilla extract and mix together. Leave the mixture to cool for 10–15 minutes.

4 Once the sugar mixture has cooled, slowly pour it into the dry ingredients with the mixer running on low speed (or use an electric hand whisk). Scrape down the sides of the bowl and then beat once more until smooth, taking care not to over mix.

5 Pour equal amounts of the cake batter into the prepared tins and bake for 20 minutes. (You can tell the sponge is cooked when it comes away from the edges of the tin slightly and a skewer comes out clean.) Leave the sponges to cool in the tins for about 20 minutes before transferring to a wire rack. Once fully cooled, use a large serrated knife to slice off the rounded dome tops so you have a level surface for stacking (see page 15).

CONTINUED OVERLEAF...

6 Make the Italian merignue buttercream according to the instructions on page 143. Very finely chop 50g (1¾oz) of the chocolate and combine with four-fifths of the buttercream to make the terrazzo buttercream. Melt the remaining 10g (⅓oz) chocolate in a microwave or in a small heatproof bowl set over a pan of barely simmering water. Place the remaining fifth of Italian meringue buttercream in a bowl and beat in the melted chocolate until smooth and evenly combined. Set aside for decorating later.

7 Stick the first sponge layer onto a cake stand or board using a small dollop of buttercream then spoon on some of the terrazzo buttercream and smooth out to the edges with an offset spatula. Repeat the process using the second layer of cake and then top with the third layer.

8 Transfer the remaining terrazzo buttercream to a piping bag and then crumb coat and fully buttercream the cake, following the steps on page 16.

9 Transfer the chocolate buttercream to a piping bag fitted with a medium round nozzle and pipe blobs of buttercream around the edge of the cake. Top each buttercream blob with a maraschino cherry.

DOUBLE PINEAPPLE UPSIDE-DOWN CAKE

This retro pineapple upside-down cake is quick and easy to make and removes the need for any extra decorating after cooking. Delicious warm or cold.

vegan butter, for greasing

1 tbsp caster (superfine) sugar

6 canned pineapple rings

100g (3½oz) canned pineapple pieces

8 maraschino cherries

165g (6oz) plain (all-purpose) flour

1 tsp baking powder

½ tsp bicarbonate of soda (baking soda)

¼ tsp fine sea salt

pinch of grated tonka bean (add 1 tsp vanilla extract to the wet ingredients if you don't have tonka)

200ml (¾ cup) condensed coconut milk

100g (3½oz) coconut oil, melted

1 Preheat the oven to 180°C/350°F/Gas 4 and line a 20cm (8in) cake tin with parchment paper then grease all over with butter and sprinkle the base with the tablespoon of sugar. Drain the pineapple rings and pineapple pieces, removing as much of the juice as possible (save this for later) then arrange the rings over the base of the tin. Drain and halve the maraschino cherries and place them in the gaps between the pineapple.

2 In a large bowl sift together the flour, baking powder, bicarbonate of soda, salt and tonka bean then set aside.

3 Pour 120ml (½ cup) of the saved pineapple juice into a separate bowl, add the coconut condensed milk and melted coconut oil and mix together.

4 Put the pineapple pieces into a food processor and blitz briefly then squeeze in a sieve to remove as much excess moisture as possible. Add this pineapple pulp to the wet ingredients and mix to evenly combine.

5 Add the wet ingredients to the dry and mix until smooth. Pour into the cake tin and smooth out the top of the batter. Bake in the oven for 40–45 minutes until golden brown on top and a skewer comes out clean. Leave to cool in the tin for about 10 minutes before running a knife around the edge of the tin and turning out onto a wire rack to cool fully.

COCONUT KITTEN

The inspiration for this cake came from a page in a 1950s edition of Good Housekeeping's *New book of Cake Decorating* (Google it – it's simultaneously amazing and terrifying). You'll need a 1 litre (2 pint) lamb mould cake tin. It's surprisingly hard to find cat-shaped cake tins so a lamb seemed to be the next best option; they are readily available online and in cake decorating shops.

FOR THE CAKE

vegan butter, for greasing

175g (6oz) plain
(all-purpose) flour

1 tsp baking powder

¼ tsp bicarbonate of soda
(baking soda)

¼ tsp salt

100g (3½oz) unsweetened
vegan yogurt

3 tbsp dairy-free milk

100g (½ cup) caster
(superfine) sugar

3 tbsp grapeseed oil

zest and juice of 2 lemons

few drops of pink food
colouring

1 tbsp psyllium husk

60g (2¼oz) fresh
raspberries

1 Preheat the oven to 180°C/350°F/Gas 4 and liberally grease the inside of your mould with butter.

2 Sift together the flour, baking powder, bicarbonate of soda and salt into a large bowl.

3 In a separate bowl mix together the yogurt, milk, sugar, oil, lemon zest and juice and pink food colouring until smooth. Add the psyllium husk and mix to combine, then add the raspberries and mix again to evenly combine. Pour the wet ingredients into the dry and stir gently. Transfer to the prepared mould and bake for 35–40 minutes.

4 Meanwhile, make the buttercream according to the instructions on page 142 or 143. Add the lemon zest and pink food colouring and mix until evenly combined; set aside.

5 Check to see if the cake if fully cooked through by testing if a skewer inserted comes out clean – the ripeness of the raspberries can affect the cooking time. If not return to the oven for a further 10 minutes. Remove and leave the cake to cool in the tin for about 15 minutes before unmoulding and transferring to a wire rack.

CONTINUED OVERLEAF...

FOR THE LEMON BUTTERCREAM

275g (9½oz) buttercream (American or Italian meringue; see pages 142–3)

zest of 1 lemon

few drops of pink food colouring

FOR THE LEMON SYRUP

45g (1½oz) caster (superfine) sugar

2 tbsp lemon juice

TO DECORATE

60g (2¼oz) pink shredded coconut (see page 152), or use uncoloured

small amounts of white, pink, green or dark brown royal icing for the face and ears (see page 22)

large coconut flakes

6 Combine the ingredients for the lemon syrup in a small bowl. While the cake is still warm, gently prick the main body all over with a fork then brush with the syrup, avoiding the head. Leave to cool fully.

7 Once completely cool, transfer your cake to a cake stand or board. Carve off the nose of the lamb to create a flatter, more 'cat-like' face. Cover the whole cake with a generous layer of buttercream using an offset spatula to make a rough, fluffy texture (you really don't need to be too neat here). Create two buttercream peaks for the ears and a little buttercream tail on the cake stand or board. Next, cover the entire buttercream layer with the pink shredded coconut. To do this, fill the palm of your hand with a generous amount of the shredded coconut and gently press onto the cake, gathering up any coconut that falls off and press on again. Take particular care around the ears.

8 For the face, use a small amount of royal icing in small piping bag fitted with a no. 1 or 2 round nozzle and draw on the eyes, nose and ears. Using scissors, cut the large coconut flakes into very thin long strips to make the whiskers and then push into each cheek of the cat's face.

ALMOND & HAZELNUT DACQUOISE

I love Yorkshire forced rhubarb and I particularly love poached rhubarb and the way it looks like fluorescent pink sticks of Blackpool rock. Somewhat surreally, it's harvested in darkened sheds by candlelight. It's in season from January to March in the UK, although you can sometimes still find it in shops in April. You can make this dessert with the later green/red rhubarb too; it just won't look quite as pretty.

FOR THE MERINGUE

110g (4oz) ground almonds

75g (2½oz) ground hazelnuts

160ml (5½fl oz) water

6g (¼oz) potato protein

pinch of xanthan gum

pinch of bicarbonate of soda (baking soda)

225g (8oz) caster (superfine) sugar

FOR THE POACHED RHUBARB

250g (9oz) caster (superfine) sugar

250ml (1 cup) water

1 vanilla pod, split lengthways and seeds scraped out

400g (14oz) forced rhubarb, trimmed and cut into 5cm (2in) batons

FOR THE WHIPPED CREAM

1 batch of whipped cashew cream (see page 146)

zest of 1 orange

1 tsp orange blossom water

100g (3½oz) icing (confectioners') sugar

1 Preheat the oven to 170°C/340°F/Gas 3 and line 2 or 3 large baking sheets with parchment paper (how many you need will depend on the size of your baking sheets). Mark out three circles on the paper that are 17cm (6in) in diameter.

2 Evenly spread the ground almonds and hazelnuts over one of the baking sheets and place in the oven for about 12 minutes until lightly golden and fragrant. Transfer to a bowl and leave to cool. Reduce the oven temperature to 120°C/250°F/Gas ½.

3 To make the meringue put 85ml (3fl oz) of the water, the potato protein and xanthan gum in a small bowl and whisk together, then place in the fridge for 30 minutes to rehydrate the potato protein. Once hydrated, add to the bowl of a stand mixer fitted with the whisk attachment (or use an electric hand whisk) and mix on a high speed for about 5 minutes.

4 Put the sugar and remaining 75ml (5 tbsp) water into a pan and place over a medium heat. Cook until the mixture reaches 110°C/230°F. Reduce the speed of the mixer to medium-high. Continue cooking the syrup until it reaches 118°C/244°F, then quickly remove the pan from the heat and, with the mixer still running, slowly trickle the syrup into the potato protein mix. Beat the mixture until it has returned to room temperature.

CONTINUED OVERLEAF...

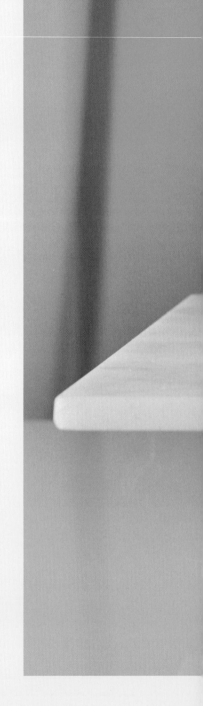

5 Tip the cooled ground nuts into the meringue and gently fold together using a spatula. Transfer the mixture to a piping bag fitted with a medium round nozzle. Then, starting from the centre, pipe spirals of meringue onto your baking sheets using the marked out circles to guide you. Bake the three meringue circles in the oven for about 1 hour.

6 To poach the rhubarb, put the sugar, water, scraped out seeds and vanilla pod into a large pan and stir together. Place over a medium heat and bring to the boil. Remove from the heat and add the rhubarb. Make a 'lid' for the rhubarb by cutting a circle of parchment paper the same diameter as the pan and place it on top of the rhubarb, then cover the pan with an actual lid. Leave to cool until the pan returns to room temperature.

7 Make the whipped cashew cream according to the instructions on page 146. Add half the orange zest, the orange blossom water and icing sugar and whip until smooth and fully combined.

8 Once both the rhubarb and meringue have cooled you can begin assembling (do this just before you want to serve). Cut the rhubarb into 5cm (2in) pieces. Place a layer of meringue on your serving plate, smooth over a third of the whipped cream, then arrange a third of the poached rhubarb pieces on top. Repeat until everything is used up. Finish by sprinkling the top layer with the remaining grated orange zest.

CASSATA SICILIANA

This is definitely a cake for those with a sweet tooth. Candied and glacé fruits can be hard to get hold of but check your local market – I found a great stall in Leeds market (The Nut Shop for anyone local to the area) which sells a selection by the gram so you don't have to buy more than you need. Failing that, you can easily buy online too.

FOR THE SPONGE

vegan butter, for greasing

300g (2¼ cups) plain (all-purpose) flour

150g (1¼ cups) potato flour

2 tsp baking powder

½ tsp fine sea salt

220g (generous 1 cup) caster (superfine) sugar

160ml (5½fl oz) grapeseed oil

250ml (1 cup) almond milk

FOR THE FILLING

160g (5½oz) raw cashews, soaked in cold water for at least 3 hours

100g (3½oz) coconut cream

65g (2½oz) caster (superfine) sugar

60g (2¼oz) coconut oil, melted

1 tsp vanilla extract

3 tbsp lemon juice

70g (2½oz) vegan dark chocolate

90g (3oz) chopped candied fruit

1 Preheat the oven to 180°C/350°F/Gas 4. Grease and line a 30 x 20cm (12 x 8in) shallow baking tin with parchment paper. Dust a 17cm (7in) pie dish with icing sugar.

2 Start by preparing the marzipan according to the instructions on page 140. Lightly dust a worktop with icing sugar and knead the marzipan for a minute or so, then add a couple of drops of food colouring and knead again until the colour is evenly distributed. Dust the worktop with icing sugar once more then roll out the marzipan into a circle about 30cm (12in) in diameter and a few millimetres (⅛in) thick. Drape the rolled marzipan over your rolling pin and then lift and drape it over the pie dish, rolling the pin out from underneath as you do so. Work quickly to push the marzipan into the corners and sides then trim the marzipan neatly around the top edge of the dish.

3 To make the sponge, in a large bowl sift together the flour, potato flour, baking powder and salt. In a separate bowl mix together the sugar, oil and milk. Pour the wet ingredients into the dry and mix until smooth. Pour into your lined baking tin and bake in the oven for 10–12 minutes. Leave to cool in the tin for a few minutes before transferring to a wire rack to cool completely.

4 To make the filling, add the soaked drained cashews and coconut cream to a blender and blitz until smooth and no graininess is left. Then add the sugar, melted coconut oil, vanilla and lemon juice and blitz once more until smooth. Finely chop the chocolate and candied fruit into small chunks, add to the mix and stir until everything is evenly distributed. Chill in the fridge while you prepare the rest of the cake.

CONTINUED OVERLEAF...

TO ASSEMBLE

380g (13oz) marzipan (see page 140 for homemade)

2 drops of green food colouring

30g (1oz) vegan dark chocolate

3 tbsp rum

200g (7oz) icing (confectioners') sugar, plus extra for dusting

juice of 1 lemon

selection of candied and glacé fruits (you can use whatever you like here; I use candied kumquats, citron, angelica, pineapple, a whole candied satsuma and a maraschino cherry)

5 Melt the 30g (1oz) chocolate for assembling and brush all over the inside of your marzipan. Slice the cooled sponge into two even layers. From one of the halves cut a 17cm (7in) circle and place this on the base of the pie dish. Then cut a 20cm (8in) circle from the other half and set aside. Use the remaining sponge to cut small fingers to line the side of the cake. Line these up all around the edges of the pie dish, making sure there are no gaps. When finished, brush the sponge all over with rum.

6 Remove the filling from the fridge and spoon the mixture into the pie dish on top of the sponge. Smooth out the top with a offset spatula, then top with the larger circle of sponge and brush with the remaining rum. Place back in the fridge for at least 3 hours for the filling to firm up.

7 When the cake has chilled, remove from the fridge and turn out onto a cake stand or board. Mix the icing sugar, lemon juice and a tablespoon of water (you may need more) together in a small bowl. You want a thick icing that won't spread very much. Use around three-quarters of this icing to cover the top of the cake, carefully smoothing out with a palette knife. Put the remaining icing into a piping bag and use to pipe swags or whatever design you like (see page 22) over the sides of the cake. Leave the icing to set for around 10 minutes then top the cake with the candied fruits in a pretty and even pattern.

8 Serve immediately or return to the fridge to chill if serving at a later point.

STRAWBERRY, OLIVE OIL & PISTACHIO MOUNTAIN CAKE

I love pistachios and would go as far to say that they are the queen of nuts, although this may just be due to the fact that I really like their colour. You can buy pistachio paste ready-made, but if you have a high-speed blender you can simply blitz pistachios yourself until smooth. The strawberries on this cake are best placed on the cake just before serving to avoid any slippage, but the rest of the cake can be prepared ahead of time.

FOR THE SPONGE
vegan butter, for greasing

280g (9¾oz) plain (all-purpose) flour

40g (1½oz) cornflour (cornstarch)

1½ tsp bicarbonate of soda (baking soda)

½ tsp salt

270g (9½oz) strawberries

240g (8½oz) caster (superfine) sugar

2 tbsp lemon juice

90ml (3fl oz) extra virgin olive oil

1 tsp apple cider vinegar

1½ tbsp psyllium husk

65ml (2fl oz) oat milk

1 Preheat the oven to 180°C/350°F/Gas 4 and grease and line three 15cm (6in) cake tins with parchment paper.

2 In a large bowl sift together the flour, cornflour, bicarbonate of soda and salt. Set aside.

3 Add the strawberries to a food processor and blitz until smooth. Transfer to a bowl and add the sugar, lemon juice, olive oil and apple cider vinegar and stir together. In a separate, small bowl mix together the psyllium husk and oat milk. Then stir this into the strawberry mixture.

4 Add the wet ingredients to the dry and combine, then pour evenly between the three prepared baking tins. Bake in the oven for 15–18 minutes then leave to cool in the tins for 5 minutes before placing on a wire rack to cool completely.

5 Meanwhile, make the Italian meringue buttercream according to the instructions on page 143 then add the strawberry powder and mix together. When the sponges have completely cooled, evenly slice each into two so you have six layers of cake. Stack the cakes up on top of each other as neatly as possible and carve the cakes into a domed shape (you shouldn't need to remove too much sponge to do this, just carve from the top three layers).

CONTINUED OVERLEAF...

TO DECORATE

550g (1¼lb) Italian meringue buttercream (see page 143)

1 tbsp freeze-dried strawberry powder

80g (2¾oz) pistachio paste

180g (6oz) strawberry jam (jelly)

600–800g (1¼–1¾lb) fresh strawberries

6 Place the bottom layer of the sponge on your cake board or stand and spread with a thin layer of pistachio paste, then a layer of buttercream. Follow with another layer of sponge, spread this with a layer of buttercream and then a layer of strawberry jam. Continue stacking the cakes with the two alternating filling combinations until you reach the final sponge layer. Crumb coat the cake (see page 16) with buttercream and leave to chill in the fridge for at least 3 hours.

7 When the cake is chilled, cover in the second layer of buttercream, I use a palette knife to dollop on small amounts of buttercream and then spread it out in different directions to create a rough looking texture for the strawberries to adhere to.

8 When ready to serve, hull and halve the strawberries and then place them cut side down on a piece of kitchen paper or a clean dish towel for a couple of minutes to absorb some of the juice. Starting from the bottom, arrange the strawberries cut side up in rows around the cake. Finish by adding a whole strawberry upside-down on the top of the cake.

MAGRITTE APPLE CAKE

René Magritte is one of my favourite artists and, as he often used apple and sky motifs in his surrealist paintings, it felt only right to cover this apple cake in a Magritte-inspired, dream-like sky blue buttercream. With its subtly spiced sponge filled with salted caramel, this cake is simply a dream.

FOR THE SPONGE

vegan butter, for greasing

100ml (3½fl oz) grapeseed oil

115g (4oz) golden caster (superfine) sugar

75g (2½oz) soft light brown sugar

475g (1lb) apple sauce (see page 149 for homemade)

1½ tsp vanilla extract

175g (6oz) plain (all-purpose) flour

20g (¾oz) cornflour (cornstarch)

1½ tsp bicarbonate of soda (baking soda)

¼ tsp fine sea salt

1 tsp ground cinnamon

¼ tsp ground nutmeg

TO DECORATE

1 batch of Italian meringue buttercream (see page 143)

2 drops of blue food colouring

150g (5oz) vegan salted caramel (see page 148 for homemade)

pinch of sea salt

silver lustre spray

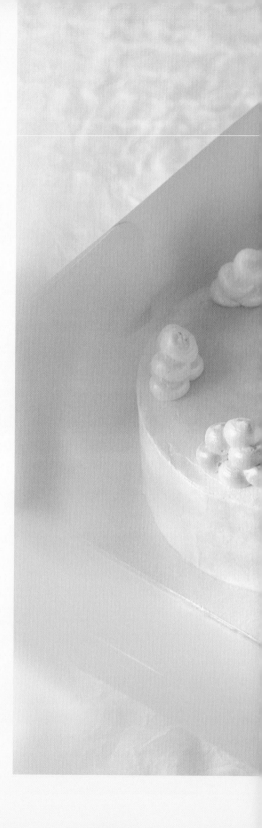

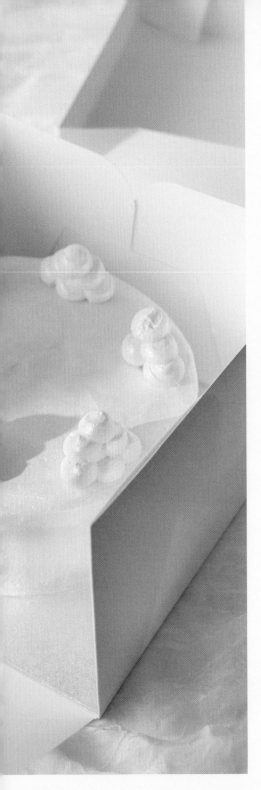

1 Preheat the oven to 180°C/350°F/Gas 4 and grease and line the base of two 20cm (8in) cake tins with parchment paper.

2 Put the oil and sugars into the bowl of a stand mixer fitted with the paddle attachment (or use an electric hand whisk) and beat until it forms a light emulsion, then add the apple sauce and vanilla and mix until combined.

3 In a separate bowl sift together all the dry ingredients, then add to the wet ingredients and beat until smooth, scraping down the sides of the bowl midway through to ensure everything is incorporated. Pour the batter equally between the prepared baking tins and bake for 25–30 minutes, or until a skewer comes out clean. Leave to cool in the tins for 10 minutes before turning out onto a wire rack to cool completely.

4 Make the Italian meringue buttercream according to the instructions on page 143. Place about one-sixth of the buttercream in a small bowl, add the blue food colouring and stir to combine. Set aside. Add the remaining buttercream to a piping bag.

5 Place the bottom layer of sponge on a cake board or stand, securing it with a blob of buttercream. Pipe a thin layer of buttercream over the sponge and smooth out using an offset spatula. Pipe a dam round the edge (see page 16) then fill with the caramel. Sprinkle the caramel with a little extra salt then top with the second layer of sponge. Crumb coat the cake (see page 16) then place in the fridge for at least 6 hours to firm up.

6 Remove the cake from the fridge and fully cover with another layer of buttercream. Then, with your palette knife, remove small scoops of buttercream around the cake, making sure you don't go through to the crumb coat layer. Using a clean palette knife, fill in holes you've just created with the blue buttercream, then smooth over with a cake scraper to achieve a watercolour 'cloud' effect.

7 Use the remaining white buttercream to pipe clouds around the top of the cake: use a medium round nozzle and pipe clusters of small blobs to achieve the cloud effect. Finish by covering the whole cake in a spritz of silver shimmer spray. This cake is best served cold from the fridge.

FANCY

BAKES

PANDAN ENGLISH MADELEINES

Not to be confused with French madeleines or Australian lamingtons, these little cakes are typically made with a light vanilla sponge that is coated in berry jam, then rolled in desiccated coconut and topped with a cherry. I make these in dariole moulds, which you can easily find online, but you can also use cupcake trays if you wish – you just might have a little sponge mixture left over.

MAKES 12

FOR THE SPONGE

vegan butter, for greasing

135g (generous 1 cup) plain (all-purpose) flour

2 tsp baking powder

¼ tsp fine sea salt

1½–2 ripe mangoes

50ml (2fl oz) grapeseed oil

100g (3½oz) caster (superfine) sugar

½ tsp pandan extract

FOR THE GLAZE

5g (¼oz) powdered pectin

100g (½ cup) caster (superfine) sugar

100ml (scant ½ cup) water

½ tsp pandan extract

TO DECORATE

120g (4oz) green shredded coconut (see page 152), or use uncoloured

80g (2¾oz) vegan butter

2 drops of pandan extract

120g (4oz) icing (confectioners') sugar

12 pieces of candied angelica (optional)

1 Preheat the oven to 180°C/350°F/Gas 4 and grease 12 dariole moulds or a 12-hole cupcake tray.

2 Sift the flour, baking powder and salt into a bowl and set aside.

3 Peel and de-stone your mangoes then blitz the flesh in a food processor until you have a smooth purée. Weigh out 260g (9oz) of the purée and place this in a large bowl with the oil, sugar and pandan extract. Mix with a spatula, then add the dry ingredients and stir again until combined.

4 Spoon equal amounts of the cake batter into your moulds, then bake in the oven for 12–15 minutes. Remove from the oven and leave to cool in the moulds for a couple of minutes before removing and transferring to a wire rack.

5 Meanwhile, make the glaze. Sift the powdered pectin and sugar into a small pan, add the water and pandan extract and stir continuously over a medium heat for about 5 minutes until the mixture thickens, then remove from the heat.

6 To glaze the cakes, use a fork to pick each one up from the underside, then dip into the pan of glaze, coating the cake completely, then place back onto the wire rack. When all the cakes are glazed, gently roll them in the shredded coconut.

7 To make the buttercream, add the butter, pandan extract and icing sugar to the bowl of a stand mixer fitted with the paddle attachment (or use an electric hand whisk) and beat until the buttercream is light and fluffy. Add to a piping bag fitted with a medium star nozzle and pipe a swirl of buttercream onto each madeleine. Top with a small piece of candied angelica to finish them off, if you like.

PINK FAT TUESDAY BUNS

Fat Tuesday buns, or semlor as they're more commonly known, are traditional Scandinavian buns that are made every year during Lent and usually eaten on Shrove Tuesday and, oh my, I think they may be one of my favourite confections of all time. A sweet cardamom bun filled to the brim with marzipan and custard then topped with whipped cream; they're so dreamy you'll be wanting to swap your pancakes for these from now on. I've also added a little extra raspberry compote to this version, which is not so traditional but very delicious.

MAKES 6

FOR THE DOUGH

50g (1¾oz) vegan butter

125ml (½ cup) full-fat oat milk

7g (¼oz) dried yeast

25g (¾oz) caster (superfine) sugar

175g (6oz) strong white bread flour

¼ tsp fine sea salt

½ tsp baking powder

1 tsp ground cardamom

FOR THE RASPBERRY COMPOTE

80g (2¾oz) raspberries

20g (¾oz) caster (superfine) sugar

1 tsp lemon juice

1 Melt the butter in a small pan, then remove from the heat and stir in the oat milk. Use a thermometer to take the temperature; you want it to be about 37°C/98°F so if it's too low place back on the heat for a few seconds and if it's too hot leave to cool slightly. This is a tepid, 'hand-hot' temperature so, if you don't have a thermometer, test by dipping in your finger – it should feel just warm. When you have the right temperature, add the yeast, stir, then add the sugar and stir again. Set aside for about 10 minutes for the yeast to activate and form a layer of bubbly foam on top.

2 Sift the flour, salt, baking powder and cardamom into the bowl of a stand mixer fitted with the dough hook attachment (or use an electric hand whisk), then pour in the yeast mixture and beat together on a low speed until fully combined. Then turn up the mixer to medium-high and beat for about 5–6 minutes. Cover the bowl with a dish towel and leave in a warm spot to prove for about 30 minutes, or until doubled in size.

3 To make the raspberry compote, put all the ingredients into a pan, stir, then place over a medium heat for 5–7 minutes, stirring occasionally, until the raspberries have broken down and the compote has thickened slightly. Remove from the heat and leave to cool.

CONTINUED OVERLEAF...

FOR THE FILLING

100g (3½oz) marzipan (see page 140 for homemade)

1–2 tbsp vegan custard (see page 147 for homemade)

FOR THE MILK WASH

2 tbsp dairy-free milk

20g (¾oz) golden (corn) syrup

FOR THE WHIPPED CREAM

300g (10½oz) whipped cashew cream (see page 146)

1 tsp vanilla bean paste

1 tbsp freeze-dried raspberry powder

icing (confectioners') sugar, for dusting

4 If using homemade, make the marzipan according to the instructions on page 140 and the custard according to the instructions on page 147, then leave to cool.

5 When the dough has doubled in size, tip onto a well floured surface and knead for a minute or two, then cut into 6 equal pieces (about 60g/2oz each). Roll into balls, making sure to tuck any straggly bits underneath. Place on a baking sheet lined with parchment paper, evenly spaced, lightly cover with a dish towel and leave to rise in a warm spot for another 25–30 minutes.

6 While the buns are proving, preheat the oven to 200°C/400°F/Gas 6 and mix together the ingredients for the milk wash. Brush all over the tops of the proven buns. Bake in the oven for 8–10 minutes, then remove and immediately cover with a dish towel to stop the buns forming a crust.

7 Once the buns have cooled completely, neatly cut a small triangle or circle from the top of each bun about 1cm (½in) in diameter. Put the tops safely to one side to use later. Scoop out around one-third of the inside of each bun and put the crumbs into a bowl.

8 Grate the marzipan into a separate bowl, add the custard and about half the scooped out crumbs and mix together until smooth. Carefully spoon this marzipan mixture evenly into the hollowed out buns, followed by a spoon of the raspberry compote.

9 Make the whipped cream according to the instructions on page 146 then stir in the vanilla bean paste and freeze-dried raspberry powder. Spoon into a piping bag fitted with a large French star tip and pipe a swirl of cream on top of each bun.

10 Top the cream with the reserved bun tops and finish with a dusting of icing sugar.

LIQUORICE & WHITE CHOCOLATE MINI CAKES

A Scandinavian-inspired flavour combination, these treacly, liquorice-scented sponges are topped with creamy white chocolate ganache and they have even converted some liquorice-phobes. They are similar to parkin, in that they get softer and stickier after they've been left in a tin for a couple of days.

MAKES 10–12

FOR THE CAKE

135g (generous 1 cup) plain (all-purpose) flour

1¼ tsp baking powder

¼ tsp salt

130g (4½oz) soft liquorice

145ml (5fl oz) oat milk

105g (3½oz) vegan butter, plus extra for greasing

2 tbsp lemon juice

130g (4½oz) caster (superfine) sugar

1 Preheat the oven to 180°C/350°F/Gas 4 and grease a silicone cupcake tray or individual mini cake moulds.

2 In a bowl sift together the flour, baking powder and salt.

3 Put the liquorice, oat milk, butter, lemon juice and sugar into a pan and place over a medium heat until the sugar has dissolved and the liquorice has softened around the edges slightly. Pour the liquorice mixture into a food processor and blitz until smooth. Pour this mixture into the bowl of dry ingredients and mix until smooth and combined.

4 Pour equal amounts of cake batter into the prepared cupcake tray or moulds and bake in the oven for 10–12 minutes.

5 To make the white chocolate ganache, place the cocoa butter in a heatproof bowl set over a pan of just simmering water and heat until melted. Add the maple syrup, stir and set aside.

CONTINUED OVERLEAF...

FOR THE WHITE CHOCOLATE GANACHE

80g (2¾oz) cocoa butter

95g (3oz) maple syrup

160ml (5½fl oz) oat milk

3 tbsp cornflour (cornstarch)

80g (2¾oz) vegan butter

2 tsp vanilla extract

pinch of salt

TO DECORATE

liquorice powder, for dusting

10 liquorice sweets

6 Put the oat milk and cornflour into a small pan, stir together and place over a low heat, whisking constantly until the mixture has thickened. Remove from the heat and set aside to cool slightly.

7 Put the butter, vanilla and salt into the bowl of a stand mixer fitted with the paddle attachment (or use an electric hand whisk) and beat until light and fluffy. Scrape down the sides of the bowl and then continue beating while you slowly pour in the cocoa butter mixture. Mix until combined then pour in the oat milk mixture and then beat again until you have a smooth ganache. Transfer to a bowl and place in the fridge for at least 30 minutes to firm up.

8 When the ganache has set slightly, give the mixture a quick stir then transfer to a piping bag fitted with a Russian ruffle tip or a petal tip. Pipe a swirl of ganache onto each cake. Dust with a sprinkling of liquorice powder and top with a liquorice sweet.

STICKY TOFFEE PYRAMIDS

If you can't get your hands on pyramid moulds then a cupcake tray will work just fine. These little puddings are the ultimate comfort food. Serve drenched in sticky toffee sauce.

MAKES 12

FOR THE CAKE

200g (7oz) pitted medjool dates, chopped

150ml (5fl oz) oat milk

85g (3oz) vegan butter, plus extra for greasing

1 tbsp golden (corn) syrup

2 tbsp treacle (molasses)

125g (generous ½ cup) soft light brown sugar

150g (1¼ cups) self-raising flour

¼ tsp fine sea salt

½ tsp mixed spice

1 tsp bicarbonate of soda (baking soda)

FOR THE SAUCE

160g (¾ cup) soft light brown sugar

1½ tbsp treacle (molasses)

3 tbsp golden (corn) syrup

25g (¾oz) vegan butter

100ml (scant ½ cup) oat cream

TO DECORATE

gold lustre dust (optional)

2 sheets of gold leaf (optional)

1 Lightly grease your pyramid or cupcake moulds.

2 Put the pitted dates into a bowl and cover with boiling water. Leave for at least an hour until the dates have softened, then drain off any excess liquid and blitz in a food processor until you have a smooth paste. Preheat the oven to 180°C/350°F/Gas 4.

3 Put the oat milk, butter, syrup, treacle and brown sugar into a pan and place over a medium heat, stirring until the sugar has dissolved. Leave to cool for 10–15 minutes then add the date mixture and stir until smooth.

4 In a separate bowl sift together the flour, salt, mixed spice and bicarbonate of soda. Add the wet mix to the dry ingredients and mix together until you have a smooth batter. Pour equal amounts into the prepared moulds and bake for 15–18 minutes.

5 While the cakes are baking you can start making the sauce. Put all the ingredients into a pan and heat over a medium-low heat, stirring continuously. Bring to the boil and cook for a further minute or so, then remove from the heat.

6 Pour the sticky toffee sauce over each cake and finish with a spray of gold shimmer and/or a fleck of gold leaf on top of each cake, if you like.

CHOCOLATE BROWNIES

I've tasted a lot of dreadful vegan brownies in my time; some that were dry and should have been labelled chocolate cake and others that tasted far too healthy. I was completely disillusioned about brownies until I purchased one in particular from Brick Lane food market in London and it was everything a brownie should be (I really wish I'd taken note of the bakery's name, to give them due credit). Inspired, I came up with my own recipe: it's super-fudgy with molten chunks of chocolate and a delicate crispy top.

MAKES 12

25g (¾oz) ground flaxseed

110ml (½ cup) dairy-free milk

200g (7oz) vegan dark chocolate (at least 70% cocoa solids)

150g (5oz) vegan butter, plus extra for greasing

150g (¾ cup) golden caster (superfine) sugar

150g (¾ cup) soft light brown sugar

1½ tsp vanilla extract

140g (generous 1 cup) plain (all-purpose) flour

60g (2¼oz) cocoa powder

½ tsp fine sea salt

1½ tsp baking powder

150g (5oz) vegan milk or dark chocolate chunks

½ tsp flakes sea salt

1 Preheat the oven to 180°C/350°F/Gas 4. Grease and fully line a 30cm (12in) square baking tin with parchment paper, making sure the paper comes up over the edges of the tin (this will make it easy to remove from the tin later).

2 Add the flaxseed and milk to a small bowl, stir and leave to thicken for about 10 minutes.

3 Melt the dark chocolate in the microwave, or in a heatproof bowl set over a pan of just simmering water, then set aside. Melt the butter in a large pan, then remove from the heat and add the sugars, vanilla, flaxseed mixture and the melted chocolate and mix until combined.

4 Sift the flour, cocoa powder, salt and baking powder together into a large bowl then add this to the wet mixture and mix until smooth.

5 Add the chocolate chunks to the batter and mix to disperse the chocolate evenly. Pour the mix into the lined baking tin, sprinkle the top evenly with the flaked sea salt and bake for 30–35 minutes. Remove from the oven (the batter will seem undercooked in the middle and will deflate once removed but, don't worry, this is supposed to happen). Leave to cool in the tin for 20–30 minutes, then transfer to a wire rack and leave to cool completely before cutting into rectangles.

CHOCOLATE CHIP COOKIES

This recipe is adapted from the Ovenly Secretly Vegan chocolate chip cookie recipe, which is a pretty great recipe: chewy in the middle, packed full of chocolate and with a light, crisp exterior. But I wanted something with a little bit more crunch around the edge for this cookie, and an extra hit of caramelly-molasses flavour. If you don't want to bake all your cookies at once you can freeze the cookie dough before baking. Just skip placing the dough in the fridge and store the shaped cookies in an airtight container in the freezer, placing parchment paper between each layer so that they don't stick together. The dough will last up to a month in the freezer. You will also need to add a couple of minutes to the cooking time when baking from frozen.

MAKES 16

250g (2 cups) plain (all-purpose) flour

¾ tsp bicarbonate of soda (baking soda)

½ tsp fine sea salt

200g (1 cup) soft light brown sugar

40g (1½oz) soft dark brown sugar

110ml (scant ½ cup) grapeseed oil

75ml (3fl oz) oat milk

1 tsp vanilla extract

225g (8oz) vegan chocolate buttons or chunks

1 In a large bowl sift together the flour, bicarbonate of soda and salt.

2 Put the sugars, oil, milk and vanilla into the bowl of a stand mixer fitted with the paddle attachment (or use an electric hand whisk). Beat for 2–3 minutes until the mixture forms a smooth, light emulsion.

3 Add the dry ingredients and beat again until incorporated, making sure you don't over-mix. Scrape down the sides of the bowl then add the chocolate buttons or chunks and use a spatula to evenly combine. Cover the bowl with clingfilm (plastic wrap) and place in the fridge for at least 6 hours or overnight to firm up.

4 Once the dough has chilled, preheat the oven to 180°C/350°F/Gas 4 and line 2 large baking sheets with parchment paper.

5 Portion the dough into 16 balls, each about 55g (2oz). Flatten them slightly and place on the lined trays spaced well apart. Bake for 12–14 minutes (depending on how chewy/crunchy you like your cookies). Leave to cool on the trays for about 5 minutes before transferring to a wire rack.

MEXICAN WEDDING COOKIES

Here in the UK I think these would officially be classed as a biscuit, but I'm going to stick with their traditional name to stop things getting confusing. These bite-sized melt-in-the-mouth cookies are really simple to make. My version of the recipe uses pecans but you can substitute other nuts if you prefer.

MAKES 24

120g (4oz) pecans

230g (8oz) vegan butter

320g (11oz) icing (confectioners') sugar

1½ tsp vanilla extract

270g (generous 2 cups) plain (all-purpose) flour

½ tsp fine sea salt

1 Preheat the oven to 170°C/340°F/Gas 3 and line a couple of baking sheets with parchment paper.

2 Spread the pecans over one of the lined baking sheets and bake in the oven for 10–12 minutes, turning the nuts halfway though toasting. Remove from the oven and allow to cool slightly, then transfer to a food processor and blitz until you have a rough, sand-like texture. Turn off the oven.

3 Put the butter, 70g (2½oz) of the icing sugar and the vanilla extract into the bowl of a stand mixer fitted with the paddle attachment (or use an electric hand whisk) and beat until light and fluffy.

4 In a separate bowl stir together the blitzed pecans, flour and salt. Add this to the butter mixture and beat again until combined.

5 Divide the dough into 24 balls, each about 25g (1oz), and place evenly spaced on the lined baking sheets (12 per sheet). Chill in the fridge for at least an hour before baking.

6 Preheat the oven to 180°C/350°F/Gas 4 then bake the cookies for 15 minutes. Put the remaining 250g (8½oz) icing sugar into a large bowl. When baked, remove the cookies from oven (they should still be quite pale) and immediately roll them in the icing sugar. Transfer to a wire rack to fully cool then roll the cookies in the icing sugar once more.

TERRAZZO PEANUT CHOCOLATE BARS

These bars sit somewhere between a rice crispy cake and a Snickers bar. They are super-rich and are packed full of toasted nuts and all kinds of salty, sweet deliciousness. Check the ingredients on your peanut butter; if it already contains salt you won't need to add any more.

MAKES 12

FOR THE PUFFED RICE LAYER

50g (1¾oz) vegan butter, plus extra for greasing

115g (4oz) golden (corn) syrup

115g (4oz) peanut butter

½ tsp salt (optional)

115g (4oz) puffed rice

FOR THE CHOCOLATE LAYER

60g (2¼oz) flaked (slivered) almonds

40g (1½oz) chopped peanuts

½ tsp fine sea salt

300g (10½oz) vegan dark chocolate (at least 70% cocoa solids)

100g (3½oz) coconut cream

1 tsp vanilla extract

1 Preheat the oven to 170°C/340°F/Gas 3 and grease and fully line a 900g (2lb) loaf tin with parchment paper, making sure the paper comes over the edges of the tin.

2 In a large pan, melt the butter over a low heat then add the golden syrup, peanut butter and salt (if using) and stir until smooth. Remove from the heat and then add the puffed rice and mix until fully combined.

3 Pour the mixture into the lined tin and press down until you have a flat, even surface. Place in the fridge to chill.

4 Line a baking sheet with parchment paper and spread the flaked almonds, chopped peanuts and salt over it. Bake in the oven for about 12 minutes until lightly toasted. Leave to cool.

5 Melt the chocolate in the microwave or in a heatproof bowl set over a pan of just simmering water. When it has fully melted, add the coconut cream and vanilla and mix until evenly combined. Add the cooled nuts and mix again to evenly distribute everything.

6 Remove the tin of puffed rice from the fridge, checking that the rice layer feels firm, then pour the nutty chocolate over the top and even out using a greased spatula. Return to the fridge to chill for at least 2 hours before lifting out of the tin and cutting into slices. (To get a nice sharp edge use a hot knife to cut into slices.)

BASIC CUT-OUT BISCUITS

This recipe for crisp and light vanilla biscuits is really great for cutting into intricate designs and shapes as it doesn't spread when baked. You can also add extra flavourings to your dough like citrus zest, spices, cocoa powder or fruit powders. I like to sandwich the biscuits together with buttercream, caramel or jam, or decorate them with royal icing (as pictured).

MAKES ABOUT 24

180g (6oz) vegan butter

150g (¾ cup) caster (superfine) sugar

1 tbsp psyllium husk

40ml (1½fl oz) oat milk

2 tsp vanilla extract

300g (2¼ cups) plain (all-purpose) flour, plus extra for dusting

¼ tsp fine sea salt

1 Put the butter and sugar into the bowl of a stand mixer fitted with the paddle attachment (or use an electric hand whisk) and beat until fluffy and evenly combined.

2 Put the psyllium husk, oat milk and vanilla into another bowl, mix and leave to thicken for a minute or so, then add to the butter and sugar mixture and beat until smooth.

3 Sift together the flour and salt in a bowl then add to the mix and beat slowly until just combined. Don't over-mix as the biscuits can become tough if the dough is over-worked.

4 Form the dough into two flat discs, wrap in clingfilm (plastic wrap) and refrigerate for 15–30 minutes. (If you don't want to bake the biscuits straight away, you can leave the dough in the fridge for 3–5 days.) Meanwhile, line 2 large baking sheets with parchment paper.

5 When the dough has chilled, lightly dust a surface with flour and roll out your biscuit dough to about 5mm (¼in) thick. Cut into any shapes you like, then place the biscuits on the lined baking sheets and place in the freezer for about 30 minutes. Meanwhile, preheat the oven to 180°C/350°F/Gas 4.

6 Bake the biscuits in the oven for 8–12 minutes until lightly golden around the edges. Leave to cool on the baking sheets for a few minutes before transferring to a wire rack.

GINGER CRACKLE BISCUITS

These molasses-packed ginger biscuits are perfectly crisp when freshly baked but turn into deliciously chewy ginger biscuits when stored in an airtight container overnight. So, if you like yours chewy, it's sadly going to require a little bit of patience. The portioned dough can be baked from frozen, just add a couple of minutes onto your baking time.

MAKES ABOUT 12

120g (4oz) vegan butter (softened)

100g (½ cup) caster (superfine) sugar

70g (generous ¼ cup) soft dark brown sugar

50g (1¾oz) treacle (molasses)

200g (1½ cups) plain (all-purpose) flour

½ tbsp bicarbonate of soda (baking soda)

¼ tsp salt

1½ tbsp ground ginger

1 tsp mixed spice

1 Preheat the oven to 180°C/350°F/Gas 4 and line 2 large baking sheets with parchment paper.

2 Add the softened butter, sugars and treacle to the bowl of a stand mixer fitted with the paddle attachment (or use an electric whisk) and beat together. Scrape down the sides of the bowl and beat again until smooth.

3 In a large bowl sift together the remaining ingredients then add this to the mix. Beat together until smooth, making sure you occasionally scrape down the sides of the bowl.

4 Divide the mixture into 12 portions, each about 45g (1½oz). Roll into balls and place 6 balls, evenly spaced, on each baking sheet. Bake in the oven for 14–16 minutes. Leave to cool on the baking sheets for about 5 minutes before transferring to a wire rack.

PISTACHIO & CHERRY FLORENTINES

This recipe makes a pretty chunky and chewy Florentine. You could temper the chocolate for this recipe but it's such a small amount that it's not worth the faff. I store these in the fridge, which makes the chocolate firm up and go matt anyway.

MAKES 12

neutral-tasting oil (such as grapeseed)

45g (1½oz) chopped pistachios

40g (1½oz) glacé cherries

65g (2½oz) flaked almonds

zest of 1 lemon

70g (generous ¼ cup) caster (superfine) sugar

2 tbsp single oat cream

35g (1¼oz) golden (corn) syrup or vegan honey

120g (4oz) vegan chocolate (use a mix or pick your favourite)

1 Preheat the oven to 170°C/340°F/Gas 3 and grease a silicone cupcake tray with a neutral-tasting oil.

2 Roughly chop the pistachios and cherries and place in a heatproof bowl along with the flaked almonds and lemon zest, then set aside.

3 Put the sugar, oat cream and syrup or honey into a pan and stir to combine. Place over a medium heat, stirring occasionally, until the mixture reaches 118°C/245°F on a sugar thermometer. If you don't have a sugar thermometer use a clean spoon to drop some of the syrup into a glass of cold water. The sugar should form a soft, flexible ball then will then flatten out after a moment. This is called the firm ball stage. Remove from the heat and pour over the pistachios and cherries. Stir until evenly combined.

4 Spoon equal amounts of the mixture into your cupcake tray (taking care as the mixture will be very hot). Cover the back of a rubber spatula with neutral-tasting oil and press the mixture down to get it as flat as possible. Bake for 12–15 minutes. Remove from the oven and leave to cool in the tray completely before turning out and setting aside.

5 Melt the chocolate in the microwave or in a heatproof bowl set over a pan of just simmering water. You can either drizzle the chocolate over the Florentines or, as I like to do, spoon a generous teaspoon of melted chocolate into each hole of the clean silicone cupcake tray, then place the Florentines on top with the neat side facing up. Push down a little and then place in the fridge for 1 hour (or the freezer for about 15 minutes) until the chocolate has set. Pop them out of the silicone tray and enjoy.

CHERRY CRÈME FRAÎCHE SCONES

I've always had a thing for the lurid colour of maraschino cherries and their syrupy sweet almond flavour. But if you're not a maraschino cherry enthusiast like I am you can leave them out of this recipe and it will still work just fine.

MAKES 12–14

450g (1lb) self-raising flour, plus extra for dusting

½ tsp salt

100g (3½oz) vegan butter, cubed

95g (½ cup) caster (superfine) sugar

265ml (9fl oz) vegan crème fraîche (I use Oatly)

½ tsp apple cider vinegar

2 tsp vanilla extract

100g (3½oz) maraschino cherries, thoroughly drained and roughly chopped

FOR THE GLAZE

2 tbsp oat milk

1 tbsp golden (corn) syrup

1 Preheat the oven to 220°C/425°F/Gas 8 and line 2 baking sheets with parchment paper.

2 Put the flour, salt, cubed butter and sugar into the bowl of a stand mixer fitted with the paddle attachment and beat on a medium speed until the mixture forms a very fine breadcrumb texture. Alternatively, rub the butter into the dry ingredients using your fingertips until you've achieved this breadcrumb texture.

3 In a separate bowl mix the crème fraîche, apple cider vinegar and vanilla.

4 With the mixer on low (or using a wooden spoon), slowly pour the wet ingredients into the dry and beat until just combined. Scrape down the sides of the bowl, then add the chopped cherries and beat once more until cherries are evenly dispersed.

5 Tip the scone mixture out onto a well floured surface and roll out to a thickness of 4–5cm (1½–2in). Use a floured 4cm (1½in) round cutter to cut out traditionally shaped scones, or use a sharp knife to cut the dough into even triangles as I have done here. Space them evenly on the baking sheets (the scones with spread quite a bit, so don't sit them too close together).

6 Mix the ingredients for the glaze together in a small bowl and use to brush the tops of the scones. Bake for 10–12 minutes until golden brown on top. Leave to cool slightly before serving.

NECTARINE BAKEWELLS

This recipe is a summer take on the classic cherry Bakewell tart. When making the compote for this recipe you want to ensure your fruits are really ripe as it will give a lot more flavour to the tart.

MAKES 12

12 blind baked small sweet shortcrust pastry cases (see page 154)

250g (9oz) nectarine compote (see rhubarb compote method on page 150 for homemade)

25g (¾oz) flaked (slivered) almonds

150g (5oz) American or Italian meringue buttercream (see pages 142–3)

zest of 1 orange

2 drops of orange food colouring

12 slices of nectarine

12 gold dragees (optional)

FOR THE FRANGIPANE

80g (2¾oz) vegan butter

100g (½ cup) golden caster (superfine) sugar

zest of 1 lemon

65ml (2fl oz) water

pinch of potato protein

pinch of xanthan gum

pinch of bicarbonate of soda (baking soda)

40g (1½oz) plain (all-purpose) flour

½ tsp baking powder

¼ tsp fine salt

180g (6oz) ground almonds

1 Preheat the oven to 180°C/350°F/Gas 4. Make 12 blind baked small pastry cases according to the instructions on page 154 then place them on a baking sheet lined with parchment paper.

2 To make the frangipane, put the butter, sugar and lemon zest into the bowl of a stand mixer fitted with the paddle attachment (or use an electric hand whisk). Beat on a medium speed until light and fluffy and everything is fully mixed.

3 In a small bowl whisk together the water, potato protein, xanthan gum and bicarbonate of soda then rest in the fridge for 30 minutes. In another bowl sift together the flour, baking powder, salt and ground almonds.

4 Remove the protein liquid from the fridge, add to the butter and sugar mixture and beat until combined. Add the almond mixture and beat once more, scraping down the sides of the bowl halfway though, then continue mixing until smooth.

5 Place a heaped teaspoon of the nectarine compote in each pastry case and smooth out, then top with a tablespoon of the frangipane. Smooth out the frangipane, sprinkle with the flaked almonds and bake for 25–30 minutes until golden.

6 Remove from the oven and leave to cool while you prepare the buttercream according to the instructions on pages 142–3. Add the orange zest and food colouring and beat again until smooth. Transfer to a piping bag fitted with a medium French star nozzle and pipe a blob of buttercream on top of each tart. Top each with a nectarine slice and gold dragee.

MELBA BOOBS

My first memories of Melba tarts are from when I was about six or seven. They were sold in a popular Yorkshire bakery and came in a selection of different pastel colours. From what I remember the main flavours were peach, pineapple and raspberry. Sadly that bakery shut down and I never saw a Melba tart again until I moved to Glasgow to study. At which point I realized that Scotland was the true home of these tarts; they are sold in most bakeries and the most common flavour is pineapple. Here is my vegan version (nipple decoration optional...).

MAKES 12

12 blind baked small sweet shortcrust pastry cases (see page 154)

300g (10½oz) pineapple or rhubarb compote (see page 150 for homemade)

150g (5oz) Italian meringue buttercream (see page 143)

pinch of grated tonka bean (use 1 tsp vanilla extract if you don't have tonka)

TO DECORATE

250g (9oz) icing (confectioners') sugar

a few drops of food colouring in your preferred colour

2–3 tbsp lemon juice (or use pineapple or berry juice)

10g (⅓oz) fondant

12 dragees

1 Make 12 pastry cases according to the instructions on page 154. If using homemade, make your preferred compote according to the instructions on page 150. Place a heaped teaspoon of compote in the bottom of each pastry case and smooth out.

2 Make the buttercream according to the instructions on page 143 then stir in the grated tonka bean. Transfer the buttercream to a piping bag and snip the tip to make a 1cm (½in) opening. Pipe a tall swirl of buttercream over the jam, making sure you completely cover the jam without covering any of the pastry case. Use a palette knife to smooth the buttercream into a neat dome then run your thumb neatly around the pastry edge to make a small groove between the pastry shell and the buttercream (this is to stop the icing from running over).

3 Sift the icing sugar into a bowl, add 2 drops of food colouring, then add the lemon juice a little at a time (you may not need all of it). You want the icing to be quite thick so it doesn't run straight off the buttercream. Spoon the icing over the buttercream domes and gently shake the tarts to make the icing run down the sides, covering all the buttercream.

4 Mix the fondant with a drop of food colouring. Divide and roll into 12 small balls and then flatten slightly to make the areolas. Stick on top of the tarts and finish with a dragree on each for the nipple.

IT

ESSERTS

PASSIONFRUIT MERINGUE PIE

Passionfruit curd adds a sharp and fragrant twist to the classic version of this pie.

SERVES 6

FOR THE PIE

1 blind baked 20cm (8in) sweet shortcrust pastry case (see page 154)

1 batch of passionfruit curd (see page 151 for homemade)

40g (1½oz) vegan white chocolate

FOR THE ITALIAN MERINGUE

4g (¼oz) potato protein

pinch of xanthan gum

140ml (5fl oz) water

pinch of bicarbonate of soda (baking soda)

200g (1 cup) caster (superfine) sugar

1 Make the pastry case according to the instructions on page 154. If using homemade, make the passionfruit curd according to the instructions on page 151.

2 Put the potato protein, xanthan gum and 5 tablespoons of the water into a small bowl, whisk together and then place in the fridge to rehydrate for 30 minutes.

3 Melt the chocolate in a microwave, or a heatproof bowl set over a pan of just simmering water, then brush the chocolate all over the inside of the pastry case. Place in the fridge to set.

4 Place the rehydrated potato protein and the bicarbonate of soda in the bowl of a stand mixer fitted with the whisk attachment (or use an electric hand whisk) and whip the mixture for about 5 minutes on high speed.

5 Meanwhile, put the sugar and remaining water into a pan placed over a medium heat; do not stir. Heat until it reaches 110°C/230°F (test with a sugar thermometer). Reduce the speed on the mixer to medium-high. Continue cooking the sugar syrup until it reaches 118°C/245°F, then quickly remove from the heat and slowly pour the syrup into the mixing bowl while whisking continuously. When all of the sugar syrup is combined, increase the speed back to high and continue beating the meringue until the bowl is cool to the touch.

6 Remove the pastry case from the fridge and fill with the passionfruit curd in a smooth layer. Top with the cooled meringue – you can do this by spooning the meringue on top of the curd or by placing the meringue in a piping bag fitted with a medium round nozzle and piping small blobs in concentric circles, building up in layers until all the meringue is used up.

7 To brown the meringue I use a blowtorch, but if you don't have one, slide the tart briefly under a hot grill (broiler) to brown the top – keep a close eye on it though!

BAKED HONEY CHEESECAKE

You may not know that it was actually the ancient Greeks who invented cheesecake. Although the texture of this dessert is reminiscent of a New York-style cheesecake, it takes some inspiration from more traditional cheesecake ingredients, with the addition of walnuts and vegan honey. Pictured on page 101.

SERVES 8

FOR THE BASE

55g (2oz) walnuts

40g (scant ¼ cup) caster (superfine) sugar

40g (scant ¼ cup) soft light brown sugar

70g (2½oz) plain (all-purpose) flour

¼ tsp baking powder

⅛ tsp salt

50g (1¾oz) vegan butter, melted, plus extra for greasing

FOR THE FILLING

150g (5oz) sultanas (golden raisins)

50ml (2fl oz) brandy

230g (8oz) raw cashews, soaked in cold water for at least 3 hours

90g (3oz) blanched almonds, soaked in cold water for at least 3 hours

500ml (2 cups) vegan crème fraîche (I use Oatly)

90g (3oz) vegan honey (or use agave or maple syrup), plus extra for drizzling

zest of 1 lemon, plus 4 tbsp juice

2 tbsp psyllium husk

2 tsp vanilla extract

1 tsp salt

few sprigs of fresh thyme, to decorate

1 Preheat the oven to 190°C/375°F/Gas 5 and grease and line the base of a 17cm (7in) springform or loose-bottomed tart tin with parchment paper.

2 To make the base, blitz the walnuts in a food processor until finely chopped. Transfer to a bowl along with the rest of the dry ingredients and stir to combine. Add the melted butter and mix again to bring everything together. Transfer to the lined tin and press down so you have an even layer then bake in the oven for 12 minutes. Place the tin on a wire rack to cool (do not remove the base from the tin).

3 To make the filling, begin by placing the sultanas in a bowl with the brandy and microwave or heat in a pan for a minute or so until the sultanas are plump and have soaked up the brandy. Roughly chop the sultanas and leave to one side.

4 Drain the soaked cashews and almonds then add to a food processor with the crème fraîche and blitz until smooth. Add the honey, lemon zest and juice, psyllium husk, vanilla and salt and blitz again until smooth. Transfer to a bowl and stir in the sultanas. Pour the mix on top of the cheesecake base and bake in the oven for 45–50 minutes.

5 Remove from the oven and allow to cool completely in the tin before removing. Drizzle with honey and decorate with thyme sprigs before serving.

ROSE & GINGER CHEESECAKE

This super-creamy cheesecake has just a light rose fragrance (no soapiness here), which is balanced out by a warming ginger biscuit base. You'll want to serve this cheesecake just after removing from the tin as the glaze won't hold up for a prolonged period.

SERVES 6–8

FOR THE BASE

200g (7oz) ginger biscuits (see page 81 for homemade)

50g (1¾oz) vegan butter, melted

zest of 1 lemon

FOR THE CHEESECAKE

200g (7oz) raw cashews, soaked in cold water for at least 3 hours

125g (4oz) coconut cream

80g (2¾oz) caster (superfine) sugar

75g (2½oz) refined coconut oil, melted

4 tbsp lemon juice

1 tsp vanilla extract

75g (2½oz) rose Turkish delight, finely chopped

1 Line a 15cm (6in) springform or loose-bottomed tart tin with parchment paper. Put the biscuits into a food processor and blitz until you have a gravelly texture (or place in a freezer bag and carefully bash with a rolling pin), then transfer to a bowl along with the melted butter and lemon zest and mix together. Tip the mixture into the prepared tin and press down so you have an even surface. Refrigerate to set.

2 To make the filling, blitz the drained cashews in a food processor along with the coconut cream until smooth and no graininess is left. Add the sugar, melted coconut oil, lemon juice and vanilla, blitz once more to combine, then transfer to a bowl.

3 Finely chop the Turkish delight then add to the cheesecake filling, stirring to evenly distribute. Spoon the mixture on top of the chilled base then tap the tin on the worktop a few times to even out the surface. Leave to chill for at least 8 hours or overnight.

CONTINUED OVERLEAF...

FOR THE ROSEWATER GLAZE

100g (½ cup) caster (superfine) sugar

8g (¼oz) powdered pectin

100ml (scant ½ cup) water

1 tbsp rosewater

3 drops of pink food colouring

TO DECORATE

100g (3½oz) Turkish delight, cubed

4 Once the cheesecake has fully chilled and you're nearly ready to serve, it's time to make the rosewater glaze. Put the sugar and powdered pectin into a small pan and whisk together. Add the water, rosewater and pink food colouring and mix until fully incorporated. Place over a medium-low heat and keep stirring until the glaze becomes fully translucent and has thickened. To test whether the glaze has thickened enough, pull the whisk out of the mixture; the glaze should form solid droplets on the wires of the whisk. Remove from the heat and then gently pour over the chilled cheesecake. Make sure to pour all over and not just from one point otherwise you may melt the cheesecake layer.

5 Return the cheesecake to the fridge for about 15 minutes to set the glaze. When fully chilled, remove the cheesecake from the tin: place the cake tin on top of a can then use a blowtorch to gently heat the sides of the cake tin (alternatively use a knife that has been dipped in hot water and run it around the edge of the tin), then slowly pull down the sides of the tin. Use a cake slice to transfer the cheesecake onto a serving plate.

6 Decorate with cubes of Turkish delight.

PERSIAN LIME PIE

This recipe is essentially a key lime pie, however key limes are often pretty hard to come by. The most common type of limes that we buy in the UK are Persian limes, hence the name for this pie. Make sure your condensed coconut milk and coconut cream have both been chilled overnight before making this recipe as it will vastly speed up the time you need to let this firm up at the end.

SERVES 8–10

FOR THE CRUST

250g (9oz) vegan digestive biscuits

85g (3½oz) vegan butter, melted

40g (1½oz) vegan white chocolate

FOR THE FILLING

300g (10½oz) chilled coconut cream

zest of 4 limes, plus 4 tbsp lime juice

250ml (1 cup) condensed coconut milk (chilled)

TO DECORATE

200g (7oz) coconut cream (chilled)

20g (¾oz) icing (confectioners') sugar

pinch of small fresh mint leaves or crystallized mint

zest of 1 lime

1 Preheat the oven to 180°C/350°F/Gas 4.

2 Put the biscuits into a food processor and blitz (or place in a freezer bag and carefully bash with a rolling pin) until you have fine crumbs, then transfer to a bowl and combine with the melted butter.

3 Press the biscuit mixture into a 18–20cm (7–8in) loose-bottomed tart tin, pushing it evenly over the base and up the sides of the tin. Bake in the oven for 10–12 minutes. Leave to cool in the tin, then transfer to the fridge to chill.

4 Once the crust is chilled, melt the white chocolate in the microwave, or in a heatproof bowl set over a pan of just simmering water. Paint the inside of the pie crust all over with the chocolate and then return it to the fridge to set.

5 To make the filling, put the chilled coconut cream into the bowl of a stand mixer fitted with the whisk attachment (or use an electric hand whisk) and beat until all the lumps have gone and the cream is fluffy.

6 Put the lime zest and juice and condensed coconut milk into a separate bowl and mix until smooth. Fold this mixture into the whipped coconut cream, then pour into the pastry case. Refrigerate for about 6 hours, ideally overnight.

7 To decorate, whip up the coconut cream with the icing sugar. Add to a piping bag fitted with a medium petal nozzle and pipe wiggles of the cream all the way around the edge of the tart. Finish with mint leaves and a scattering of lime zest.

TIRAMISU

When making this I couldn't quite work out a way to make a vegan savoiardi (ladyfinger) biscuit, but the light, soft sponge that takes its place does a good job of soaking up the Marsala and coffee without becoming a soggy mess. If you can't get your hands on Marsala then you can substitute with sherry or even red vermouth.

SERVES 6
You will need 6 dessert glasses about 7cm (2½in) in diameter

FOR THE CASHEW CREAM
100g (3½oz) raw cashews, soaked in cold water for at least 3 hours

3 tbsp dairy-free milk

35g (1¼oz) soft light brown sugar

45g (1½ oz) caster (superfine) sugar

¼ tsp fine sea salt

50g (1¾ oz) refined coconut oil, melted

1 tbsp Marsala

300g (10½oz) full-fat coconut cream

FOR THE SPONGE
135ml (generous ½ cup) almond milk

1 tsp apple cider vinegar

1 tsp vanilla extract

125g (generous ½ cup) caster (superfine) sugar

80g (2¾oz) vegan butter

100g (scant 1 cup) plain (all-purpose) flour

45g (1½oz) potato flour

1 tsp baking powder

½ tsp bicarbonate of soda (baking soda)

¼ tsp fine sea salt

TO ASSEMBLE
150ml (5fl oz) freshly brewed strong coffee

75ml (3fl oz) Marsala

15g (½oz) cocoa powder

1 Begin by making the cashew cream. Drain the cashews and blitz in a food processor with the milk, sugars, salt, melted coconut oil and Marsala until smooth. Whip the coconut cream in a mixer fitted with the whisk attachment (or use an electric hand whisk) for 2 minutes until light and fluffy. Fold the cashew mixture into the coconut cream until combined, then chill in the fridge.

2 Now make the sponge. Preheat the oven to 180°C/350°F/Gas 4 and grease and line a 30 x 20cm (12 x 8in) cake tin. Put the milk, vinegar and vanilla into a small bowl, stir and set aside to thicken. Beat the sugar and butter in a clean mixer fitted with the paddle attachment (or use an electric hand whisk) until light and fluffy. Sift the remaining dry ingredients together in a separate bowl.

3 With the mixer on medium-low speed, add the milk mixture and sifted dry ingredients alternately in small batches until everything is fully combined and smooth. Pour into the cake tin and bake for 15 minutes. Leave to cool in the tin for a few minutes then turn out onto a wire rack to cool fully.

4 Combine the coffee and Marsala in a small bowl. When your cake is fully cooled, use a pastry cutter to cut out 12 circles, about 7cm (2½in) in diameter. Place a circle of cake in each dessert glass and brush with the coffee soak, making sure to saturate the sponge (how much you use will depend on how much coffee flavour you like). Put the chilled cashew cream into a piping bag and cut a 2cm (¾in) hole in the end. Pipe an even layer of cream on top of the sponge and dust with cocoa powder.

5 Repeat with the second layer of sponge, soaking with the coffee and Marsala as before and finishing with a layer of cashew cream, smoothing the top. Dust the top with cocoa powder, using a stencil if you like. Serve straight away or chill in the fridge until you're ready to serve.

PRALINE TOFU MOUSSE

These are small but very rich, so don't be
disappointed by the size of the portion.
They're also really quick to put together and,
don't worry, you won't actually taste any tofu.

SERVES 6
You will need 6 dessert glasses about
7cm (2½in) in diameter

FOR THE PRALINE MOUSSE
70g (2½oz) vegan white chocolate

220g (8oz) silken tofu

⅛ tsp salt

90g (3oz) praline paste (see page 131)

**FOR THE CHOCOLATE
MOUSSE**
70g (2½oz) vegan dark chocolate

130g (4½oz) silken tofu

⅛ tsp salt

1 tsp vanilla extract

15g (½oz) soft light brown sugar

1 For the praline mousse, melt the white chocolate in
a microwave or a heatproof bowl set over a pan of just
simmering water. Add to a food processor along with the
rest of the ingredients and blitz until smooth, scraping down
the sides of the bowl occasionally to make sure everything is
incorporated. Divide the mixture between 6 dessert glasses
and place in the freezer for 10 minutes to set the mousse.

2 Repeat the method above to make the chocolate
mousse. Remove the serving glasses from the freezer and
gently top with the chocolate mousse. Eat straight away or
chill in the fridge until ready to serve.

TRIFLE

Jelly or no jelly? This can be the cause of some debate when it comes to trifle. Here I've decided to say 'yes' to jelly, albeit one that is meltingly soft-set, sherry-spiked and dotted with peaches. It sits beneath layers of tart berry compote, soft vanilla cake, whipped cream and custard. This recipe can be made year round by simply leaving out the fresh raspberries and swapping fresh peaches for canned in winter, which incidentally adds an extra retro feel to this classic dessert.

SERVES 6–8

FOR THE SPONGE

100g (½ cup) caster (superfine) sugar

115g (scant 1 cup) self-raising flour

15g (½oz) cornflour (cornstarch)

¼ tsp fine sea salt

1 tsp baking powder

70g (2½oz) vegan butter (at room temperature)

65g (¼ cup) unsweetened vegan yogurt

65ml (2fl oz) dairy-free milk

1 tsp vanilla extract

FOR THE JELLY

150ml (5fl oz) sherry

50ml (2fl oz) water

30g (1oz) caster (superfine) sugar

¼ tsp agar agar powder

1 large peach

1 Preheat the oven to 190°C/375°F/Gas 5 and grease and line the base of a 20cm (8in) cake tin with parchment paper.

2 To make the sponge, sift the dry ingredients into the bowl of a stand mixer then add the butter. With the paddle attachment fitted (or using an electric hand whisk), beat together on a low-medium speed until the mixture resembles fine breadcrumbs. Whisk together the yogurt, milk and vanilla in a separate bowl, then pour this over the breadcrumb mix and beat again on a low speed until combined. Scrape down the sides of the bowl and beat once more on a medium-high speed for about 2 minutes until light and fluffy. Transfer the cake batter to the lined cake tin and bake for 20–25 minutes. Leave to cool in the tin for a few minutes before turning out onto a wire rack to cool completely.

CONTINUED OVERLEAF...

FOR THE COMPOTE

400g (14oz) frozen mixed berries

135g (4½oz) caster (superfine) sugar

juice of 1 lemon

FOR THE CUSTARD

45g (1½oz) cornflour (cornstarch)

70g (2½oz) caster (superfine) sugar

500ml (2 cups) oat milk

1 vanilla pod, split lengthways,
or 2 tsp vanilla bean paste

TO ASSEMBLE

3 tbsp sherry

150g (5oz) fresh raspberries

330g (11½oz) whipped cashew cream
(see page 146)

50g (1¾oz) icing (confectioners')
sugar

freeze-dried raspberry powder,
for dusting

3 To make the jelly, put the sherry, water and sugar into a pan then sprinkle over the agar agar and leave to rehydrate for 15 minutes. Peel, core and chop the peach into small cubes. When the agar agar has hydrated, place the pan over a medium heat, bring to the boil and simmer for 2 minutes. Remove from the heat and pour into the bottom of your trifle dish, then scatter with the chopped peaches. Leave to cool to room temperature before transferring to the fridge.

4 To make the compote, put all the ingredients into a pan and place over a medium heat. Stir the mixture frequently until the sugar has dissolved and the fruit has begun to break down, then cook for a further 5 minutes, stirring frequently. Remove from the heat and leave to cool.

5 To make the custard, put the cornflour, sugar and a splash of the milk into a small bowl and mix together until you have a smooth paste. Pour the remaining milk into a pan. Scrape out the seeds from the vanilla pod and add to the pan along with the pod (or use vanilla bean paste). Place over a medium heat and bring to a simmer. Remove the vanilla pod, then add the cornflour mixture, whisking constantly until the mixture has thickened. Remove from the heat, cover the top of the custard with a sheet of parchment paper to stop a skin forming and leave to cool.

6 When everything has cooled you can begin assembling your trifle. Gently spoon about two-thirds of the compote on top of the jelly and smooth out. Brush the underside of your sponge all over with the sherry. Place it soaked side up on top of the compote (depending on the size of your trifle dish you may need to trim the sponge to fit).

7 Transfer the cooled custard to the bowl of a stand mixer (or use an electric hand whisk) and whip for around 2 minutes until smooth (it's important you do this step otherwise you'll end up with a blancmange-like layer in your trifle). Spoon the custard on top of the sponge and smooth out. Stir the fresh raspberries into the remaining compote and spoon this on top of the custard layer.

8 Make the whipped cashew cream according to the instructions on page 146 then beat in the icing sugar. Spoon this on top of the trifle then dust liberally with raspberry powder. Serve straight away or chill in the fridge until needed.

BERRIES & CREAM FLOWER JELLY

Agar agar jellies have quite a different texture and mouth-feel to jellies set with gelatine – you won't get quite the classic wibble wobble but they still taste delicious. If you can't get a hold of any edible flowers you could try adding some sliced strawberries or freeze-dried fruit pieces. This jelly has three layers: a berry layer at the bottom, then a cream layer, then a flower layer, so if you are making this in a mould (which will be inverted), you'll need to start with the flower layer.

SERVES 8

FOR THE FLOWER LAYER

250ml (1 cup) elderflower cordial

300ml (1¼ cups) water

1 tbsp lemon juice

½ tsp agar agar powder

selection of edible flowers

FOR THE CREAM LAYER

250ml (1 cup) oat milk

2 tsp vanilla extract

1 tsp freeze-dried strawberry powder

35g (1¼oz) caster (superfine) sugar

¼ tsp agar agar powder

FOR THE BERRY LAYER

300g (10½oz) frozen mixed berries

180ml (¾ cup) water

1 tbsp lemon juice

120g (generous ½ cup) caster (superfine) sugar

1 tsp agar agar powder

1 Start by making the flower layer. Put the elderflower cordial, water and lemon juice into a pan, then sprinkle the agar agar powder over the top and mix. Leave for 15 minutes for the agar agar to rehydrate then place over a medium-low heat and bring to the boil, stirring frequently, then let simmer for 2 minutes. Remove from the heat and pour through a sieve into your heatproof jelly mould (straining the mixture stops as many bubbles forming on the surface).

2 Place the mould in a large bowl of iced water. Keep stirring the jelly as it cools; as the jelly begins to thicken slightly add the flowers, petal side down. Transfer the jelly to the fridge to set completely.

3 To make the cream layer, combine the oat milk, vanilla, strawberry powder and sugar in a pan and sprinkle over the agar agar powder. Leave to rehydrate for 15 minutes, then cook as before, bringing to the boil and letting it simmer for 2 minutes. Transfer to a bowl or jug and cool slightly by placing in a bowl of iced water, then strain the cream layer over the first flower layer (making sure the flower layer has set) and return to the fridge until set.

4 For the berry layer, put the frozen berries, water, lemon juice and sugar into a food processor and blitz until smooth. Press the mixture through a sieve into a pan to remove any seeds and sprinkle with the agar powder, stir, then leave to rehydrate for 15 minutes. Place over a medium heat, bring to the boil and let simmer for 2 minutes. Remove from the heat, transfer to a bowl or jug and cool as before. Pour over the set cream layer then return the jelly to the fridge to set before turning out.

MUSCAT JELLIES WITH FROSTED GRAPES

This refreshing, golden soft-set jelly is perfect for when you're looking for something sweet but light. I like to serve mine in champagne saucers for an extra fancy touch.

SERVES 6
You will need 6 champagne saucers or dessert glasses

FOR THE JELLY
½ vanilla pod , split lengthways

600ml (2½ cups) Muscat wine or any sweet dessert wine

3 tbsp lemon juice

60g (2¼oz) caster (superfine) sugar

¾ tsp agar agar powder

FOR THE FROSTED GRAPES
20–25 grapes (in small bunches)

40g (1½oz) caster (superfine) sugar

1 Scrape the seeds from the vanilla pod into a large bowl, add the wine, lemon juice and sugar and whisk together to disperse the vanilla seeds. Sprinkle the top of the liquid with the agar agar powder, stir again, then set aside for 15 minutes to allow the agar agar to rehydrate.

2 Pour the liquid into a pan, place over a medium heat and bring to the boil, then reduce the heat and simmer for about 2 minutes, stirring all the time. Remove from the heat, allow to cool slightly, then strain the liquid through a sieve (this helps to stop bubbles forming on the surface) into 6 glasses then leave to cool to room temperature before placing in the fridge.

3 To make the frosted grapes, put the grapes in a bowl with a splash of water and roll them around until they are all wet. Drain off any excess water and then sprinkle over the sugar, rolling them again to coat in the sugar. Cover the bowl with clingfilm (plastic wrap) and place in the freezer to chill.

4 To assemble, simply top the jellies with the frosted grapes and serve.

GOOSEBERRY CUSTARD FOOL

Ever since I can remember my mum has made a version of this dessert whenever gooseberries are in season. I like using green gooseberries rather than red as they are tarter. This is delicious with a couple of Mexican wedding cookies on the side (see page 76).

SERVES 6

375g (13oz) green gooseberries

75g (2½oz) caster (superfine) sugar

1½ tbsp elderflower cordial

250g (9oz) chilled coconut cream

FOR THE CUSTARD

20g (¾oz) cornflour (cornstarch)

25g (¾oz) caster (superfine) sugar

160ml (5fl oz) full-fat oat milk

1 tsp vanilla bean paste

1 Top and tail the gooseberries using scissors and add to a pan along with the sugar. Place over a medium heat and cook for 10–15 minutes, stirring occasionally, until the gooseberries have broken down and most of the liquid has cooked off. You should be left with a thick compote-like consistency. Remove from the heat then strain through a fine sieve to remove the seeds. Add the elderflower cordial to the strained compote, mix and set aside to cool.

2 Put the cornflour, sugar and a splash of the oat milk into a small bowl and whisk together until you have a smooth paste. Pour the rest of the oat milk into a pan with the vanilla, place over a low heat and add the cornflour mixture. Whisk continuously until the mixture thickens, then remove from the heat, cover the top with a circle of parchment paper to stop a skin forming and set aside to cool.

3 When both the compote and custard have fully cooled, pour the chilled coconut cream into a large bowl and whip until smooth. Add the custard and mix until combined. Add around four-fifths of the gooseberry compote and mix once more until evenly combined. Divide the fool equally between serving bowls or glasses and then top with the remaining gooseberry compote.

4 Serve straight away or return to the fridge until ready to serve.

AMBROSIA SALAD

This recipe originates from South America, the main components of which are usually citrus fruits and coconut. Apart from these key ingredients there is room for personal preference – I've seen recipes with nuts, different fruits and even mayonnaise! I have based my recipe on that of the first Ambrosia salad I ever came across, which is the one from Tim Burton's film *Edward Scissorhands*.

SERVES 6–8

FOR THE AMBROSIA

350g (12oz) fresh pineapple (prepared weight)

150g (5oz) lychees

250g (9oz) maraschino cherries

1 x 298g (11oz) can of mandarin or clementine segments

1 fresh coconut

250g (9oz) chilled coconut cream

150g (5oz) mini marshmallows

TO DECORATE

150g (5oz) chilled coconut cream

1–2 drops of green food colouring

6–8 maraschino cherries (with stems)

1 Peel, core and chop the pineapple into small chunks, approximately 1–2cm (½–¾in). Peel and de-stone the lychees and chop into 1cm (½in) chunks. Drain the maraschino cherries and mandarin segments, then halve the cherries.

2 Break open the coconut, remove the outer shell then finely grate the flesh, avoiding the brown skin (you need about 100g/3½oz) grated coconut). See page 152 for more detailed instructions on how to safely break open a coconut.

3 Pour the coconut cream into a large bowl and whisk for 1–2 minutes until smooth. Add the marshmallows followed by the rest of the prepared fruits and stir together until everything is evenly incorporated. Either transfer to a large serving dish or divide between individual dishes.

4 To decorate, pour the coconut cream into a bowl, add the green food colouring and whisk the mixture until smooth. Transfer to a piping bag fitted with a medium closed star nozzle then pipe swirls on top of the ambrosia salad. Finish by topping with the maraschino cherries.

5 Serve straight away or chill in the fridge until ready to serve, although this is best eaten the day you make it.

CHEESECAKE MOCHI

These are so simple to make and you can use whatever flavour jam you like, however it's best to use a set jam as you'll need the filling to be quite firm. You can even speed up the process by using shop-bought vegan cream cheese – simply mix 70g (2½oz) vegan cream cheese with 70g (2½oz) jam and 30g (1oz) icing (confectioners') sugar and use this for the filling. Sweet or glutinous flour is available in most Asian supermarkets and can easily be found online.

MAKES 16

FOR THE MOCHI

100g (3½oz) sweet/glutinous rice flour

120g (generous ½ cup) caster (superfine) sugar

120ml (½ cup) water

drop of food colouring

cornflour (cornstarch) or potato starch, for dusting

FOR THE FILLING

35g (1¼oz) raw cashews, soaked in cold water for at least 3 hours

15g (½oz) vegan crème fraîche

20g (¾oz) refined coconut oil, melted

juice of ½ lemon

pinch of salt

70g (2½oz) set jam (jelly) of your choice

30g (1oz) icing (confectioners') sugar

1 Put the flour, sugar and water into a heatproof bowl and whisk together until smooth, then add the food colouring and mix again. Cover with clingfilm (plastic wrap) and heat in the microwave in 30-second bursts, removing the bowl and stirring with a spatula between each 30-second burst. The mixture will gradually thicken and go somewhat lumpy but don't worry; this is normal. Continue cooking until the mochi looks like a sticky dough and has become somewhat translucent (depending on the wattage of your microwave this will take between 2½–6 minutes to thicken).

2 Liberally dust a work surface with the cornflour or potato starch and tip the dough out onto it, taking care as the mochi will be very hot at this point. Dust the dough all over and then roll out to a 24cm (9in) square. Leave to cool on the surface while you make the filling.

3 For the filling, drain the cashews and add to a food processor with the crème fraîche, melted coconut oil, lemon juice and salt and blitz until smooth. Transfer the mixture to a bowl, add the jam and icing sugar and mix until smooth. Place this in the freezer for about 10 minutes to firm up.

4 Using a pizza cutter or sharp knife, cut the chilled mochi into 6cm (2½in) squares. Remove the chilled filling from the freezer and then add a heaped teaspoon of filling to the middle of each square. Pull the corners of the mochi together to conceal the filling and pinch the seams firmly to seal. Dust the bottom with a little more flour if it's a bit sticky. Place them seam side down on a plate and either serve immediately or chill in the fridge until ready to serve.

BLACK SESAME BANANA BREAD

The sesame in this recipe balances out some of the sweetness from the bananas to make this a perfect morning treat. You can use white sesame seeds here if you can't find black ones.

MAKES 8–10 SLICES

vegan butter, for greasing

300g (10½oz) very ripe bananas

4 tbsp grapeseed oil

60g (2¼oz) black tahini (see note)

150g (¾ cup) soft dark brown soft sugar

150g (1¼ cups) plain (all-purpose) flour

150g (5oz) ground almonds

½ tsp fine sea salt

1½ tsp baking powder

20g (¾oz) black sesame seeds, or use white sesame seeds

1 Preheat the oven to 190°C/375°F/Gas 5. Grease and line a 900g (2lb) loaf tin with parchment paper, ensuring the paper hangs over the tin to make it easier to remove the banana bread later.

2 Mash the bananas in a large bowl using a potato masher until smooth but not puréed (you still want a little texture left). Add the oil, tahini and sugar to the mashed banana and mix until you have a smooth emulsion.

3 Sift the flour, ground almonds, salt and baking powder together into a separate bowl to distribute the ingredients evenly. Add this to the bowl of wet ingredients and mix until you have a smooth batter. Pour into the lined loaf tin, evenly sprinkle the sesame seeds over the top of the loaf, then bake for 35–40 minutes until a skewer comes out clean.

NOTE
If you can't find black tahini then simply put 75g (2½oz) black sesame seeds into a high-speed blender and blitz until it forms a smooth paste. Add a little oil to the seeds if it's not coming together. Or, use regular tahini.

BROWN BETTY

This dessert is based on a traditional American Brown Betty. The dessert is somewhat like an English crumble but uses pieces of bread rather than flour in the topping. For this recipe I have used sourdough bread which is soaked in cinnamon, butter and sugar, then twice baked to create crunchy nuggets of cinnamon toast – delicious when paired with the tart blackberries, pears and cider. I like to serve mine with vegan cream or ice cream.

SERVES 6–8

300g (10½oz) sourdough bread, torn into 5cm (2in) pieces

100g (3½oz) vegan butter

165g (¾ cup) soft light brown sugar

½ tsp salt

1 tbsp ground cinnamon

4 pears

150g (5oz) blackberries

2 tbsp lemon juice

100ml (scant ½ cup) pear or apple cider

1 Preheat the oven to 180°C/350°F/Gas 4 and line a large baking sheet with parchment paper.

2 Put the bread pieces into a large bowl. Melt the butter in a pan over a medium heat, then remove from the heat and add the sugar, salt and cinnamon and mix until smooth. Pour this over the bread pieces and mix using your hands, working the sugar and butter into the bread. Tip onto your prepared baking sheet and bake in the oven for 30 minutes, turning occasionally to evenly cook the bread. Remove from the oven and leave to cool.

3 Increase the oven temperature to 200°C/400°F/Gas 6. Peel and chop the pears into 1cm (½in) cubes and add to a bowl along with the blackberries and lemon juice; toss together.

4 Once the cinnamon bread has cooled add half to a freezer bag and gently bash with a rolling pin to break into small breadcrumbs.

5 Place half of the fruit mixture in a square 20cm (8in) ceramic dish then cover with the fine breadcrumbs. Drizzle with half the cider and then top with the remaining fruit. Cover with the remaining large breadcrumbs and drizzle with the remaining cider. Cover the top of the baking dish with parchment paper, then a layer of foil. Bake in the oven for 40–45 minutes. Let cool slightly before serving with vegan cream or ice cream.

HAZELNUT & CHOCOLATE BOSTOCK

This French invention is a super-indulgent option for brunch. Fluffy brioche, slathered in chocolate ganache, then topped with hazelnut frangipane. This works best with day-old bread as it soaks up more of the delicious rum and vanilla syrup.

SERVES 6

6 slices of brioche, about 2.5cm (1in) thick (see page 123 for homemade)

30g (1oz) chopped hazelnuts

icing (confectioners') sugar, for dusting

FOR THE FRANGIPANE

180g (6oz) ground hazelnuts

pinch of xanthan gum

3g (1⁄16oz) potato protein

pinch of bicarbonate of soda (baking soda)

60g (2¼oz) vegan butter

50g (¼ cup) caster (superfine) sugar

50g (¼ cup) soft light brown sugar

1 tsp vanilla extract

¼ tsp fine sea salt

40g (1½oz) plain (all-purpose) flour

FOR THE CHOCOLATE SPREAD

70g (2½oz) vegan dark chocolate

40ml (1½fl oz) vegan single cream (I use Oatly)

35g (1¼oz) icing (confectioners') sugar

¼ tsp sea salt flakes

FOR THE SUGAR SYRUP

1 tbsp rum

1 tsp vanilla extract

100g (½ cup) caster (superfine) sugar

85ml (3fl oz) water

1 Preheat the oven to 180°C/350°F/Gas 4. Line a baking sheet with parchment paper and spread over the ground hazelnuts, then bake for about 8 minutes, turning halfway through cooking. Leave to cool on baking sheet.

2 To make the chocolate spread, melt the chocolate in a microwave, or in a heatproof bowl set over a pan of just simmering water. Allow to cool slightly then add the cream, icing sugar and salt and mix until smooth. Chill in the fridge.

3 To make the syrup, put all the ingredients into a pan and stir over a medium heat until the sugar has dissolved. Set aside to cool slightly.

4 To make the frangipane, put 4 tablespoons of water into a small bowl, followed by the xanthan gum, potato protein and bicarbonate of soda. Whisk together and place in the fridge to rehydrate for 30 minutes.

5 Add the butter and sugars to a mixer fitted with the paddle attachment (or use an electric hand whisk) and beat until fluffy, then add the vanilla, salt and protein powder liquid from the fridge and beat once more, scraping down the sides of the bowl. Add the toasted ground hazelnuts and flour and beat until smooth.

6 Line a baking sheet with parchment paper. To assemble the bostock, brush both sides of the brioche slices with the sugar syrup. Arrange over the baking sheet then spread the top sides with 1 tablespoon of chocolate spread followed by 3 tablespoons of frangipane and spread evenly. Finish with a sprinkling of chopped hazelnuts and bake in the oven for 25 minutes until the frangipane in golden at the edges. Dust with icing sugar before serving warm.

GOLDEN PUDDING

A gooey and comforting pudding (that you could technically eat for breakfast as it contains croissants and marmalade). You can find vegan croissants in health food stores, some large supermarkets and online.

SERVES 6

vegan butter, for greasing

6 vegan croissants

150g (5oz) marmalade

75g (2½oz) sultanas (golden raisins)

3 tbsp brandy

2 sheets of gold leaf, to decorate (optional)

FOR THE CUSTARD

68g (2½oz) golden caster (superfine) sugar

20g (¾oz) cornflour (cornstarch)

720ml (3 cups) oat milk

1 vanilla pod, split lengthways

1 Grease a 30 x 20cm (12 x 8in) ceramic or glass dish with vegan butter. Slice each croissant in half, spread one half with the marmalade and then top with the other halves to make marmalade sandwiches. Chop these into large chunks then layer in the baking dish.

2 Put the sultanas and brandy into a small bowl and heat in the microwave (or in a pan) for about 1 minute until the sultanas look plump. Drain off the excess brandy and scatter the sultanas over the croissant chunks.

3 To make the custard, put the sugar and cornflour and a splash of milk into a small bowl and stir to make a smooth paste. Put the remaining milk into a pan with the vanilla pod, place over a low heat and bring to a simmer. Add the cornflour mixture and whisk continuously until the mixture thickens slightly. Remove the vanilla pod then pour straight over the croissants. Leave the pudding to stand for about 20 minutes while you preheat the oven to 180°C/350°F/Gas 4.

4 Bake in the oven for 30–35 minutes. Leave to cool slightly then decorate with gold leaf, if you like, and serve.

BRIOCHE

The method and ingredients of this recipe bear very little similarity to a traditional brioche but the end result is a fluffy yet rich loaf that's perfect for toasting and covering with butter and jam, as well as for using in any dessert recipe that uses brioche.

MAKES 1 LOAF

320g (11oz) strong white bread flour

50g (1¾oz) potato starch

½ tsp fine sea salt

1 tsp baking powder

100g (3½oz) vegan butter, plus extra for greasing

250ml (1 cup) dairy-free milk

50g (¼ cup) soft light brown sugar

12g (½oz) active dried yeast

1 tsp vanilla extract

½ tsp orange blossom water

1 tbsp pearl sugar

FOR THE GLAZE

2 tsp golden (corn) syrup

1 tbsp dairy-free milk

1 Sift the flour, potato starch, salt and baking powder into the bowl of a stand mixer or large bowl.

2 Melt the vegan butter in a pan, then remove from the heat and stir in the milk and sugar. Use a thermometer to take the temperature; you want it to be about 37°C/98°F. If it's too low place back on the heat and if it's too hot leave to cool slightly. This is a tepid, 'hand-hot' temperature so, if you don't have a thermometer, test by dipping in your finger – it should feel just warm. Add the yeast, stir and set aside for 10 minutes for the yeast to activate and form a layer of bubbly foam on top.

3 When the yeast is ready, add the wet ingredients to the dry, along with the vanilla extract and orange blossom water. Fit the mixer with the dough attachment (or use an electric hand whisk) and mix on a low speed. When combined, increase the speed to high and beat for about 6 minutes until smooth.

4 Place the dough in a lightly greased bowl, cover with a clean dish towel and leave to prove in a warm spot for 30 minutes, or until the dough has doubled in size.

5 After the dough has proved, knock back by kneading for 1 minute then shape into a log, tucking any straggly bits of dough underneath. Grease a 900g (2lb) loaf tin and add the dough. Cover the tin with a dish towel and leave to prove in a warm spot for another 45 minutes, or until doubled in size. Preheat the oven to 190°C/375°F/Gas 5.

6 When the dough is proved, sprinkle the top with pearl sugar and bake for 20 minutes. Mix together the syrup and milk for the glaze. Remove the brioche from the oven and glaze, then return to the oven for 10 minutes. Leave to cool in the tin for 15 minutes then transfer to a wire rack to cool fully.

CINNAMON ROLLS

These lean heavily towards American-style cinnamon buns but have a Scandinavian touch of added cardamom in the dough. The rolls are drenched in cream cheese icing and are best served on the day of baking.

MAKES 9

FOR THE DOUGH

70g (2½oz) vegan butter, plus extra for greasing

250ml (1 cup) dairy-free milk

7g (¼oz) active dried yeast

30g (1oz) soft light brown sugar

320g (11oz) strong white bread flour, plus extra for dusting

½ tsp fine sea salt

1 tsp ground cardamom

FOR THE FILLING

90g (3oz) vegan butter, melted

90g (3oz) soft light brown sugar

1½ tbsp ground cinnamon

FOR THE ICING

40g (1½oz) vegan butter, softened

40g (1½oz) vegan cream cheese

½ tsp vanilla bean paste

150g (5oz) icing (confectioners') sugar

1 Grease a 30cm (12in) square tin. Melt the butter in a small pan, then add the milk and heat until warm. Use a thermometer to take the temperature; you want it to be about 37°C/98°F so if it's too low place back on the heat for a few seconds and if it's too hot leave to cool slightly. This is a tepid, 'hand-hot' temperature so, if you don't have a thermometer, test by dipping in your finger – it should feel just warm. Remove from the heat, stir in the yeast, then add the sugar and stir again. Set aside for about 10 minutes for the yeast to activate and form a layer of bubbly foam on top.

2 Sift the flour, salt and cardamom into the bowl of a stand mixer fitted with the dough hook attachment (or use an electric hand whisk), then pour in the activated yeast mixture. Mix on a low speed until combined then increase the mixer to medium-high and beat for about 6 minutes. Place the dough in a large greased bowl, cover with a dish towel and leave in a warm spot for 30 minutes, or until doubled in size.

3 While your dough is proving, make the filling. Mix the melted butter, sugar and cinnamon together until smooth.

4 Lightly dust a work surface with flour and turn out your proved dough. Knock back the dough by kneading for a minute or so, then roll it out into a large rectangle, about 1cm (½in) thick. Spoon the cinnamon mixture on top of the dough and spread evenly to cover completely. Roll up the dough from a long side into a log and trim off each end to neaten. Use a sharp knife or piece of string to evenly cut the dough into 9 pieces (I prefer to use string as it maintains the roundness of the rolls). Place the cinnamon rolls in the greased baking tin, cover with a dish towel and leave in a warm spot for another 30–40 minutes to prove a final time.

5 Preheat the oven to 200°C/400°F/Gas 6 and bake for 20–25 minutes. Remove from the oven and leave to cool in the tin.

6 To make the icing, mix together the butter, cream cheese and vanilla until smooth. Gradually mix in the icing sugar until fully combined. Remove the cooled cinnamon rolls from the tin, slather over the icing and serve.

TEMPTIN

G

TREATS

PINK PRALINES

These pink pralines originate from Lyon, France. They're used in desserts such as pink praline tart, in brioche or eaten as is. I like to use them as decoration for cakes and desserts but they also make a really pretty gift when bagged up. When making this recipe it's important you clean down your pans and utensils properly between cooking each batch of sugar so as not to burn the ingredients or cause premature crystallization of the sugar.

MAKES ABOUT 150

360g (12½oz) granulated sugar, divided into 3 equal amounts

105ml (3fl oz) water, divided into 3 equal amounts

pink food colouring

200g (7oz) whole almonds

½ tbsp orange blossom water or rosewater

1 Line a large baking sheet with parchment paper and preheat the oven to 90°C/200°F/Gas ¼.

2 Put one third of the sugar into a frying pan (skillet) with one third of the water and a few drops of pink food colouring. You'll want it to look pretty red to get a pastel colour as the end result. Stir together and place over a medium-high heat and bring the mixture to the boil. Continue cooking until large bubbles form on the surface of the sugar, then add the almonds. Stir vigorously with a spatula to coat with the sugar, then add the orange blossom or rosewater and continue stirring as the sugar begins to crystallize. When you have covered the almonds as evenly as possible, tip them out onto the baking sheet along with any of the crystallized sugar.

3 Clean the pan and spatula. When the almonds have cooled, separate any big clumps of crystallized sugar from the sugar-coated almonds and reserve for later.

4 Add the sugar-coated almonds to the cleaned frying pan, leaving the heat off for now. Add the second batch of sugar and water to a separate pan, along with the reserved crystallized sugar clumps and a drop of pink colouring. Stir over a medium-high heat until the syrup reaches a temperature of 124°C/255°F. Turn on the heat under the almond pan, tip over the syrup and stir vigorously to coat the almonds; it will begin to crystallize as with the first batch. When you feel you have coated the almonds as much as possible, tip back into the baking sheet.

5 Clean your pans and utensils and separate the crystallized sugar clumps from the almonds once more. Repeat step 4 again with the remaining sugar and water. Place the baking sheet of almonds in the oven for 45 minutes to dry out. These will keep for 1–2 months in an airtight container.

SALT CARAMELS

Caramelized sugar gives a rich, deep flavour that you cannot quite get from making caramels that use ingredients like evaporated milk. If you want to get creative, then feel free to add extra flavourings. I've added pinches of cardamom, smoked salt and liquorice powder to mine in the past and they're also great when topped with toasted nuts at the end. Make sure you have all your ingredients weighed out before you start this recipe; you will need a sugar thermometer too.

MAKES ABOUT 50

400g (14oz) caster (superfine) sugar

100ml (scant ½ cup) oat cream

250g (9oz) vegan butter, cubed

1½ tsp sea salt flakes, plus extra to finish

1 Line a 900g (2lb) loaf tin with parchment paper, making sure there is nowhere for the caramel to leak from.

2 Place the sugar in a large pan over a medium heat. Let the sugar start melting then begin to stir it. The sugar will clump together and re-melt – continue stirring as more and more of the sugar melts. When all the sugar has melted down continue cooking for around 1 minute until the mixture turns a rich golden brown. Remove from the heat then quickly pour in the cream and stir (be very careful not to burn yourself at this point as the mixture is extremely hot and will bubble up and steam).

3 When the cream is fully incorporated add the butter and stir until melted. Return the caramel to the heat and continue stirring until the mixture reaches 128°C/262°F. Remove from the heat, stir in the salt (any extra flavourings should be added at this point) and pour into the lined tin.

4 Leave at room temperature to cool and set (this should take about 3 hours). Then cut into what ever size pieces you like and sprinkle with more sea salt flakes to finish.

NOTE
I store these by wrapping them individually in small squares of parchment paper and then in an airtight container. They will last for at least 6 months when stored correctly.

NUT BRITTLE

Brittle looks so pretty as decoration and is really tasty as a snack too. It can also be used to make praline paste (see below), to be added to buttercream and chocolates.

MAKES ABOUT 275G (10OZ)

200g (7oz) skinned hazelnuts (or use pecans, almonds, pistachios)

400g (14oz) caster (superfine) sugar

2 tbsp water

1 Preheat the oven to 170°C/340°F/Gas 3 and line a baking sheet with parchment paper. Spread the nuts over the lined baking sheet and bake in the oven for 12–14 minutes to toast and draw out the oils. Remove and tip onto a plate.

2 Put the sugar and water into a pan, stir to combine and place over a medium heat. Cover the pan with a lid (ideally glass, so you can see inside the pan) and let the sugar melt (do not stir). When the caramel starts to turn a golden colour around the edges, remove the lid. At this point you can swirl the pan gently, once or twice, to even out the colour.

3 When the caramel turns a rich golden colour, remove the pan from the heat and tip in the nuts. Swirl the pan so the nuts get coated, or use an oiled spatula to stir. Then pour the mixture back onto the lined baking sheet and leave to cool for about 1 hour. Break into chunks and store in an airtight container lined with parchment paper for up to a month.

PRALINE PASTE

1 batch of nut brittle (see above)

¼ tsp fine sea salt

1 tbsp grapeseed oil, if needed

1 Break up the cooled nut brittle and place in a food processor along with the salt. Blitz until smooth – this can take up to 10 minutes depending on the strength of your food processor. If it's still not coming together you can add the grapeseed oil to help the mixture along.

2 If not using the praline paste immediately, keep in the fridge in an airtight container – it will last a couple of weeks.

MERINGUE SWANS

These meringue swans look really impressive and are surprisingly simple to make once you've mastered your piping skills. I like to use seasonal fruits and flowers to decorate them, but use whatever is available to you.

MAKES 6

FOR THE MERINGUES

105ml (3fl oz) bottled water (ensures a fairly neutral pH level)

5g (⅛oz) potato protein

pinch of xanthan gum

pinch of baking powder

150g (¾ cup) caster (superfine) sugar

TO ASSEMBLE

300g (10½oz) chilled coconut cream

½ vanilla pod, split lengthways

1 tsp rosewater

25g (¾oz) icing (confectioners') sugar

400–500g (14–16oz) fresh fruits (raspberries, strawberries and blueberries work well)

15g (½oz) chopped pistachios

handful of fresh edible flowers

1 Line 2 baking sheets with parchment paper.

2 Put 55ml (2fl oz) of the water, the potato protein and xanthan gum into a small bowl, whisk together and place in the fridge for 30 minutes to rehydrate the potato protein.

3 Once hydrated, add to the bowl of a stand mixer fitted with the whisk attachment (or use an electric hand whisk) and mix on high speed for about 5 minutes.

4 Add the sugar and remaining water to a pan and place over a medium heat. Cook the sugar syrup until it reaches 110°C/230°F (do not be tempted to stir this mixture during cooking). Reduce the speed of the stand mixer to medium-high and continue cooking the syrup until it reaches 118°C/245°F, then quickly remove the pan from the heat and, with the mixer still running, slowly pour the sugar syrup into the whipped potato protein. Increase the speed back to high and beat the mixture until the mixing bowl has returned to room temperature.

5 Preheat the oven to 130°C/265°F/Gas mark ¾.

6 Transfer the meringue mixture to a large piping bag fitted with a no.4 or 5 round nozzle. Pipe the head and neck in one continuous line in a long, thin 'S' shape on the lined baking sheets, with one slightly rounded end for the head (as pictured). Repeat this 6 times. To make the wings I use lots of short upward stroke lines of varying length to create a fluffy texture. Make 6 of these facing to the left and 6 facing to the right so you can sandwich them together at the end.

7 Bake the piped swans in the oven for about 1 hour (it can take more or less depending on how thick your piping is).

8 To make the filling, whip up the coconut cream until it holds firm peaks. Scrape out the seeds from the vanilla pod and add to the cream along with the rosewater and icing sugar. Whisk until smooth.

9 Chop your chosen fruit into small pieces and stir about two-thirds of it into the cream. Place a small dollop of the cream onto each serving dish and then top with the remaining fruit. Sprinkle over the pistachios and edible flowers. Place matching swan wings on each side of the cream, squishing in a little so they stick, then add the neck. Serve immediately.

MERINGUE PILLARS

This recipe is very similar to the meringue swans on pages 132–3 but yields a bigger quantity of meringue – perfect for use as your go-to meringue recipe. You can use this meringue for piping into any shape, creating meringue nests or even just dolloping onto a baking sheet. Here I explain how to pipe some Ionic (Greek-style) pillars which you'll need to decorate the 24 carrot gold cake on page 36.

MAKES 12–18, DEPENDING ON SIZE

155ml (5½fl oz) bottled water (ensures a fairly neutral pH level)

7g (¼oz) potato protein

large pinch of xanthan gum

large pinch of baking powder

225g (generous 1 cup) caster (superfine) sugar

1 Line 2 baking sheets with parchment paper.

2 Put 80ml (2¾fl oz) of the water, the potato protein and xanthan gum into a small bowl, whisk together then place in the fridge for 30 minutes to rehydrate the potato protein.

3 Once hydrated, add to the bowl of a stand mixer fitted with the whisk attachment (or use an electric hand whisk) and mix on high speed for about 5 minutes.

4 Place the sugar and remaining water in a pan set over a medium heat. Cook the sugar syrup until it reaches 110°C/230°F (do not stir). Reduce the speed of the stand mixer to medium, continue cooking the syrup until it reaches 118°C/245°F, then quickly remove from the heat and, with the mixer still running, slowly pour the sugar syrup into the whipped potato protein. Increase the speed to high and beat until the mixing bowl has returned to room temperature.

5 Preheat the oven to 130°C/265°F/Gas ¾.

6 Transfer the mixture to a piping bag fitted with a no.4 or 5 round nozzle. Pipe 3 long vertical lines side by side onto the lined baking sheets. Now pipe a horizontal line at the top and bottom (the same width as the 3 joined vertical lines). Then, on top of these short horizontal lines, pipe another line that curls inwards at both sides (as pictured on page 133). Repeat, creating as many pillars as you can, until the meringue mixture runs out.

7 Go over all the piping once more to give the meringue extra strength, then bake for about 1 hour (it may take more or less time depending on how thick your piping was).

8 Leave to cool on the baking sheets for 10 minutes before transferring to a wire rack to cool completely.

WATERMELON & STRAWBERRY PÂTE DE FRUITS

I always thought these were really difficult to perfect before I realized that the trick is to use powdered rather than liquid pectin – thankfully now available in most big supermarkets. If you want to go the extra mile with your pâte de fruits you can buy silicone *petit four* moulds online to make them into pretty shapes. It's really important that you have everything weighed out for before you start making this recipe.

MAKES 50–75, DEPENDING ON HOW YOU CUT THEM

FOR THE PECTIN MIXTURE

40g (1½oz) caster (superfine) sugar

12g (½oz) powdered pectin

FOR THE SUGAR AND GLUCOSE MIXTURE

380g (13oz) caster (superfine) sugar

100ml (3½fl oz) glucose syrup

8ml (¼fl oz) lime juice

FOR THE FRUIT PURÉE

200g (7oz) strawberry purée (see note below)

185g (6½oz) watermelon purée (see note below)

1 tbsp lime juice

FOR THE PINK ROLLING SUGAR

350g (12oz) granulated sugar

few drops of pink food colouring

bunch of fresh mint leaves, or a drop of peppermint oil

1 Fully line a 20cm (8in) square baking tin with parchment paper. Mix together the ingredients for the pectin mixture in one bowl and the ingredients for the sugar and glucose mixture in another bowl.

2 Put both fruit purées into a large pan and place over a low-medium heat. Bring the mixture to 60°C/140°F while stirring frequently with a whisk. Add the pectin mixture, whisk to combine and bring to the boil, stirring all the time.

3 When the mixture has reached 100°C/212°F add the sugar and glucose mixture and whisk to combine, then swap to a rubber spatula to stir. Stir constantly so the mixture doesn't catch, heat for around 30 minutes until it reaches 107°C/225°F, then remove from the heat and stir in the lime juice.

4 Pour the mixture into the prepared baking tin and leave to cool at room temperature for around 6 hours or overnight.

5 To make the pink rolling sugar, stir together the sugar and food colouring until the colour has coated all the sugar evenly. Bash the mint leaves with a pestle and mortar until in tiny pieces and mix into the sugar. Spread over a large baking sheet and leave to dry out for 6 hours or overnight.

6 Chop the pâte de fruit into cubes (or whatever shapes you like). Scrunch up the pink sugar then roll the jellies in it until evenly coated. Serve straight away or store in an airtight container at room temperature for up to 2 weeks.

NOTE

To make the fruit purées simply put the given quantity of hulled strawberries or peeled and chopped watermelon into food processor and blitz until smooth, then run through a fine sieve to remove the seeds.

LOLLIPOPS

If you want to use moulds for this recipe, make sure you buy ones that can withstand high temperatures. I like to make my own moulds using food-grade silicone, which is readily available online. Another easy way of making your own moulds is to evenly spread a thick layer of cornflour (cornstarch) onto a baking sheet. Then use something like a bottle lid to make impressions in the flour, into which you will be able to gently pour the sugar syrup. This method is really effective but it will result in a cloudy surface on the lollipop. You'll also need to source some paper lollipop sticks.

MAKES 12 LARGE OR 24 SMALL LOLLIPOPS

185g (generous ¾ cup) caster (superfine) sugar

130ml (4½fl oz) glucose syrup

4 tbsp water

food colouring (optional)

few drops of flavouring (such as peppermint or vanilla extract)

TO DECORATE
gold leaf (optional)

herbs or edible flowers

1 If you're using gold leaf, place this in your moulds before making the lollipops.

2 Place all the ingredients apart from your chosen flavouring in a pan and stir. Place over a medium heat and bring the mixture to 154°C/310°F (do not stir). Once the mixture has come to temperature, very quickly remove it from the heat, stir in the flavouring, then quickly but gently pour straight into the moulds. If you're adding herbs or edible flowers, then I'd recommend half-filling the moulds, adding the flowers or herbs, then pouring over a second layer of mixture.

3 Lay the end of the paper lollipop sticks in the moulds while the mixture is still hot, giving them a little twist so they are completely covered by the mixture. Top with more gold leaf (if using) at this point.

4 Leave to set for at least 30 minutes before unmoulding. You'll need to transfer straight to individual airtight confectionery bags or an airtight container lined with parchment paper as they will get very sticky when they make contact with the air.

THE

BASICS

MARZIPAN

This is my basic recipe for marzipan, which I use to cover cakes before decorating or to make pretty cake decorations.

MAKES ENOUGH TO COVER A 20–23CM (8–9IN) CAKE

300g (10½oz) ground almonds

50ml (2fl oz) glucose syrup

225g (8oz) icing (confectioners') sugar

1 tsp almond extract (optional)

1 tbsp water

2 tbsp lemon juice

1 Put the ground almonds into a food processor and blitz for a few minutes to get them really fine.

2 Transfer the ground almonds to a stand mixer fitted with the paddle attachment (or use an electric hand whisk) followed by the glucose syrup, icing sugar, almond extract, water and lemon juice. Beat on low speed until combined, then increase the speed for a minute or so until smooth.

3 To store marzipan, wrap it tightly in clingfilm (plastic wrap) and then place inside an airtight container. It will keep for about 1 month at room temperature.

MARZIPAN PEACHES

These can be used to decorate cakes or desserts but are delicious just eaten as they are. They also make perfect gifts for marzipan lovers when packaged in a pretty box.

cornflour (cornstarch), for dusting

marzipan (see above)

orange food colouring

powdered peach colouring

powdered red or pink colouring

1 Lightly dust a work surface with cornflour. Add a couple of drops of orange food colouring to the marzipan and knead together until you have an even peach colour.

2 Tear off small portions of the marzipan (around the size of a medium strawberry) and roll into balls. Flatten the ball a little bit and then use something like a toothpick or pointed sugar modelling tool to poke a hole in the top of the peach, where the stem would be, wiggling it around a little so you have a good sized hole. Then use the toothpick to dent a crease down one side of the peach.

3 Finish by dusting on small amounts of the peach and red powdered food colouring to create a blush effect.

MARZIPAN PEARLS

These make really pretty cake decorations with minimum effort, but are also pretty great on their own to nibble on.

marzipan (see opposite)

pearl or silver shimmer dust

1 Simply tear off small pieces of marzipan, around the size of a pearl (or any size you like) and roll into balls.

2 Place the balls in a small bowl, followed by a pinch of shimmer dust, then shake the bowl around to coat the marzipan evenly.

MARZIPAN ROSES & LEAVES

These are the traditional decoration for the cherry bombe princess cake on page 38. Make in whatever size and colour you like.

cornflour (cornstarch), for dusting

marzipan (see opposite)

pink and green food colouring

small circle cutters

1 Lightly dust a work surface with cornflour. Add a few drops of pink food colouring to the marzipan and knead together until the colour is evenly dispersed.

2 Flatten out the marzipan slightly and then place in between two large sheets of parchment paper. Roll out the marzipan until it's a couple of millimetres (⅛in) thick.

3 With a small circle cutter, cut out 6 petals for each rose. Thin the edges using your fingers or place back in between the sheets of parchment paper and use the back of a spoon to thin out.

4 Roll the first circle into a tube and then pull out the top edges to define the petals.

5 Wrap the next petal around the first one and flare out the edges a little. Continue until you've added all of the petals, making sure you flare out each one to create a 'rose in bloom' effect.

6 When all of the petals are added, use a sharp knife to trim the bottom of the flower off so it can sit upright on your cake.

7 To make the leaves, repeat steps 1 and 2 using green food colouring. Use a sharp knife to cut out leaf shapes, then use a toothpick or the back of a knife to make vein marks on the surface of the leaf.

AMERICAN BUTTERCREAM

I would recommend using Naturli baking block for this recipe, or a similar product that is firm when refrigerated. Vegan spreads tend to be too soft and when used in buttercream recipes on their own they create a sloppy consistency that doesn't hold up when used in layer cakes. If you can't get your hands on baking block (or similar) then you'll need to use a mixture of vegetable fat and vegan spread to make a stable buttercream – the last thing you want after all your preparation is a cake landslide. This recipe makes enough to crumb coat and fill a 20cm (8in) three-layer cake or enough to fully cover and fill a 15cm (6in) three-layer cake.

MAKES ABOUT 1.4KG (3LB)

600g (1¼lb) chilled vegan butter (Naturli baking block or similar), cubed, or 400g (14oz) vegan spread and 200g (7oz) vegetable fat

2 tsp vanilla extract

800g (1¾lb) icing (confectioners') sugar

1 Put the cubed butter into a mixer along with the vanilla extract. Using the paddle attachment (or an electric hand whisk), beat on medium speed until the mixture is light and fluffy, about 5 minutes.

2 Turn the mixer off and add a quarter of the icing sugar. Cover the bowl with a clean dish towel (or use a mixing guard) and beat on low speed until the sugar is incorporated. Carry on adding the icing sugar in small batches until everything is mixed in. Then increase the speed to high and mix for at least 5 minutes, occasionally scraping down the sides of the bowl to ensure everything is incorporated. (The longer you beat it the better and fluffier it will get.)

3 Your buttercream is now ready for you to add any colourings or extra flavourings. Chill in the fridge until ready to use; it will keep for up to 1 week in the fridge in an airtight container.

ITALIAN MERINGUE BUTTERCREAM

This recipe requires a little more work than American buttercream and you'll need a sugar thermometer to make the syrup, but the results are well worth it. You can use soya protein if you can't get potato protein – your meringue won't hold peaks but you'll still end up with a smooth buttercream after you've added the vegan butter.

MAKES ABOUT 1.1KG (2½LB)

265ml (9fl oz) water

7g (¼oz) potato protein or soya protein

large pinch of xanthan gum

large pinch of bicarbonate of soda (baking soda)

375g (13oz) caster (superfine) sugar

500g (1lb 2oz) vegan butter (Naturli baking block or similar), chilled

2 tsp vanilla extract

⅛ tsp salt

NOTE

If your buttercream is soupy then either your meringue wasn't cool enough when you added the butter or your butter was too warm. Don't worry, this isn't the end for your buttercream. Place it in the fridge for 15 minutes and then re-whip for 5 minutes. If this doesn't work, place back in the fridge for another 15 minutes and try again. If your buttercream is curdled then it could be that the ingredients are *too* cold. In this case, place 1–2 heaped tablespoons of buttercream in a small bowl and microwave for 30 seconds or so until almost totally melted. Return this to the bowl and whip once more.

1 Put 140ml (4¾fl oz) of the water, the potato or soya protein and xanthan gum into a small bowl and whisk together. Put the bowl in the fridge for 30 minutes for the protein to rehydrate.

2 Add this liquid to the bowl of the stand mixer fitted with the whisk attachment (or use an electric hand whisk), followed by the bicarbonate of soda. Whisk the mixture for about 5 minutes.

3 Put the sugar and remaining water into a pan and place over a medium heat. Bring the mixture up to 110°C/230°F then reduce the speed on the mixer to medium-high. Continue cooking the sugar syrup until it reaches 118°C/245°F, then quickly remove from the heat and slowly pour into the mixing bowl with the machine still running. Increase the speed to high and continue beating until the bowl is cool to the touch.

4 Chop the butter into small cubes, then begin adding the butter in small quantities, beating after each addition, until it has been fully incorporated. Don't worry if the mixture looks as though it is curdling, it should come together at the end (see note).

5 Add the vanilla and salt and mix until evenly combined. Use straight away or store in the fridge in an airtight container for up to 1 week, although you should let the buttercream come up to room temperature and then re-whip if using later.

WHIPPED CASHEW CREAM

This recipe requires a little more effort than coconut whipped cream but is well worth it if you don't want a coconut flavour overtaking your desserts, or if you just aren't a fan of coconut. The result is really light and fluffy and you can easily add extra flavouring and sugar without the cream collapsing. This recipes makes a big batch that can easily be halved if needed.

MAKES ABOUT 660G (1½LB) (ENOUGH FOR THE CHERRY BOMBE PRINCESS CAKE ON PAGE 38)

120g (4oz) raw cashews, soaked in cold water for at least 3 hours

250ml (1 cup) full-fat oat milk

1 tsp vanilla extract

⅛ tsp fine sea salt

50g (¼ cup) caster (superfine) sugar

½ tsp xanthan gum

240g (8½oz) refined coconut oil, melted

1 Drain the soaked cashews thoroughly, then put into a high-speed blender along with the oat milk. Blitz until totally smooth.

2 Add the vanilla, salt, sugar and xanthan gum followed by the melted coconut oil and blitz once more until smooth.

3 Place in a bowl and refrigerate for about 3 hours to allow the coconut oil to solidify.

4 When fully chilled, add the cashew cream to the bowl of a stand mixer fitted with the whisk attachment (or use an electric hand whisk). Beat for 5–8 minutes, occasionally scraping down the sides of the bowl. The cream is done when light and fluffy. Whipped cashew cream is best used freshly whipped, as the coconut oil will re-solidify when placed in the fridge for too long.

CUSTARD

This is my basic custard recipe. I think I've got it just right but if you like your custard thicker, add a little more cornflour, or sugar if you like it sweeter.

MAKES ABOUT 560ML (1 PINT)

50g (¼ cup) golden caster (superfine) sugar

30g (1oz) cornflour (cornstarch)

500ml (2 cups) oat milk

1 vanilla pod, split lengthways

1 Put the sugar and cornflour into a bowl with a splash of the oat milk and mix into a smooth paste.

2 Pour the remaining oat milk into a pan. Scrape out the seeds from the vanilla pod and add to the pan along with the pod. Stir together and place over a low-medium heat. Bring to a simmer then turn down the heat to low. Add the cornflour mixture and whisk constantly until the mixture thickens.

SALTED CARAMEL

This recipe makes a rich, silky caramel that you're going to want to pour over everything from now on, from cakes to ice cream. You need to make sure you have everything weighed out before you begin as you'll need to add ingredients quickly.

MAKES ABOUT 435G (15OZ) (ENOUGH TO FILL A STANDARD JAM JAR)

200g (1 cup) caster (superfine) sugar

100ml (3½fl oz) oat or soya cream

135g (4½oz) vegan butter (Naturli baking block or similar), at room temperature

½ tsp sea salt flakes, or to taste

1 Put the sugar into a heavy-based pan and place over a medium heat. Let the sugar start to melt without stirring, then, as you see patches begin to caramelize, start stirring. The sugar will begin to clump and re-melt; continue stirring and eventually the sugar will all melt into caramel.

2 Remove the pan from the heat and quickly pour in the cream. Vigorously stir the mixture, being careful not to burn yourself as liquid will rapidly bubble up and spit. Continue mixing until the caramel is smooth and the bubbles have died down, then add the butter and mix again until smooth. Finish by adding the sea salt flakes.

3 Serve warm straight away or refrigerate in an airtight container for later. The caramel will thicken in the fridge so you may want to bring it back to room temperature before serving.

APPLE SAUCE

You can find apple sauce on many supermarket shelves, either in the baby food section or the 'free from' section but make sure it's unsweetened. However, it's easy to make your own. You can use pretty much any variety and colour of apple you like, but I like to use cooking apples such as Bramley.

An average apple weighs about 85g (3oz) but once peeled, cored and cooked it will reduce down. Here's some maths to help you work out how many apples you will need for your desired amount of sauce:

2 apples = 125g (4oz) apple sauce

4 apples = 250g (9oz) apple sauce

6 apples = 375g (13oz) apple sauce

1 Peel and core the apples then chop into large chunks. Add to a pan, cover with a lid and place over a low-medium heat for 10–15 minutes. They won't burn as they have a high water content. Cook until the apples are tender and translucent.

2 Transfer the cooked apples to a food processor and blitz until you have a smooth purée with no lumps.

3 Leave to cool before adding to any recipe.

CHERRY PIE FILLING

Shop-bought cherry pie filling is great and I have on occasion eaten it straight from the can with a spoon... But this recipe is even more delicious, with a great balance of tartness and sweetness. I like to use fresh cherries in season because they tend to have more flavour but you can use frozen cherries too.

MAKES ENOUGH FOR THE CHERRY BOMBE PRINCESS CAKE ON PAGE 38

200g (7oz) cherries, pitted

2 tbsp water

2 tbsp lemon juice

50g (¼ cup) caster (superfine) sugar

1 tbsp cornflour (cornstarch)

1 Put all the ingredients into a pan and stir together. Place the pan over a medium-low heat and bring the mixture to the boil. Reduce the heat to low and cook for a further 10 minutes, stirring frequently.

2 Leave to cool before storing in an airtight container in the fridge, where it will keep for up to 5 days.

PINEAPPLE COMPOTE

This compote only uses a little sugar as pineapple is pretty sweet as is. This will keep for up to 5 days when stored in an airtight container in the fridge.

MAKES ABOUT 900G (2LB)

1 medium pineapple (about 900g/2lb)

2 tbsp rum

seeds from ½ vanilla pod

50–100g (¼–½ cup) caster (superfine) sugar

1 Peel, core and chop the pineapple into large chunks – you should get about 300g (10½oz) chopped pineapple. Place two-thirds in a food processor and blitz until you have a thick pineapple mush.

2 Add the blitzed pineapple to a pan along with the rum and vanilla seeds. Stir together and place over a medium-low heat for about 20 minutes to reduce, stirring frequently. Meanwhile, chop the remaining pineapple into small dice.

3 When the pineapple looks thick and most of the liquid has cooked off, give the pineapple a taste. Add sugar depending on your preferred sweetness. Add the chopped pineapple and cook this mixture for a further 10–15 minutes until thick. Remove from the heat and leave to cool at room temperature.

RHUBARB COMPOTE

Chopping the rhubarb into small pieces makes this compote more 'stable' for use in cakes, as it reduces the amount of long fibres which can make the sponges slide around. I also use this method for making other compotes in the book, such as nectarine and strawberry.

MAKES ABOUT 550G (19OZ) (ENOUGH TO FILL A 3-LAYER 20CM/8IN) CAKE)

400g (14oz) rhubarb (or nectarine or strawberry)

130g (generous ½ cup) caster (superfine) sugar

juice of 1 lemon

1 Chop half of the rhubarb into 1cm (½in) cubes and the other half into 5mm (¼in) cubes. Place the larger cubes in a pan along with the sugar. Place over a low-medium heat and cook for about 10 minutes, stirring frequently, until most of the liquid has evaporated.

2 Add the smaller rhubarb cubes to the pan and cook for a further 5 minutes until softened. Remove from the heat, add the lemon juice and leave to cool.

3 Store in an airtight container in the fridge for up to 5 days.

PASSIONFRUIT CURD

This passionfruit curd is delicious spread on toast, sandwiched between cake layers and used in the passionfruit meringue pie recipe on page 94.

MAKES ENOUGH FOR THE PASSIONFRUIT MERINGUE PIE ON PAGE 94

9 passionfruits

160g (generous ¾ cup) caster (superfine) sugar

30g (1oz) cornflour (cornstarch)

⅛ tsp fine sea salt

80ml (2¾fl oz) dairy-free milk (choose one with a neutral taste)

3 tbsp lemon juice (from about 1–2 lemons)

50g (1¾ oz) vegan butter (Naturli baking block or similar), at room temperature, cubed

1 Halve the passionfruits, scoop out the pulp and put this into a food processor. Pulse for 30 seconds to loosen the seeds then pass the passionfruit pulp through a sieve to get 100ml (3½fl oz) juice. Reserve 1 tablespoon of the seeds and discard the rest.

2 Put the juice, reserved seeds and the remaining ingredients apart from the butter into a pan. Place over a low heat and whisk continuously until the mixture begins to thicken and becomes slightly translucent; this should take 3–5 minutes. Remove from the heat (make sure you don't overcook as the mixture will scorch) and add the cubed butter, whisking to combine.

3 Transfer the mixture to a bowl and cover the top with a circle of parchment paper, then leave to cool to room temperature before transferring to an airtight container to fully set for about 6 hours or overnight. Store in the fridge for up to a week.

COLOURED
SHREDDED COCONUT

Cracking coconuts is not something I particularly enjoy doing, and I didn't actually realize there was any particular technique until recently. Instructions below on how to attempt this without (hopefully) breaking anything else. You will need a screwdriver, or similar, and a hammer.

MAKES ENOUGH FOR THE COCONUT KITTEN ON PAGE 49 OR THE PANDAN ENGLISH MADELEINES ON PAGE 64

1 fresh coconut

few drops of food colouring

1 Preheat the oven to 180°C/350°F/Gas 4. Pierce each of the 3 holes at the top of the coconut with a screwdriver and drain out the juice.

2 Put the coconut into the oven for about 10 minutes, then remove from the oven and reduce the heat to 140°C/285°F/Gas 1.

3 Wrap the coconut in a dish towel, place it on a hard surface or the floor and whack with a hammer a few times to break it open. The coconut flesh should now easily come away from the hard shell.

4 Using a fine grater, shred the coconut flesh, avoiding the brown skin. When the whole coconut is shredded, put the flesh in a bowl with a few drops of food colouring and mix until the colour is evenly distributed.

5 Evenly spread the coconut over a baking sheet lined with parchment paper and place in the oven for 40–50 minutes to dry out, occasionally turning so the coconut doesn't catch. Allow to cool before storing in an airtight container for up to a week.

SWEET SHORTCRUST PASTRY

Normally, it's quite important to keep shortcrust pastry cold at all times. With this recipe, however, there's no need to worry as the dough should be quite warm when you roll it out and line your pastry cases; it will be too crumbly otherwise. Do make sure you freeze the dough, though, as this helps to stop shrinkage when cooking.

**MAKES 24 MINI TARTS,
12 SMALL TARTS, OR
1 X 20CM (8IN) TART/PIE**

115g (4oz) cold cubed vegan butter or coconut oil (at room temperature if using coconut oil), plus extra for greasing

200g (7oz) plain (all-purpose) flour, plus extra for dusting

¼ tsp fine sea salt

60g (generous ¼ cup) caster (superfine) sugar

1–2 tbsp ice-cold water

zest of 1 lemon or orange (optional)

1 Grease your tins liberally. Sift the flour, salt and sugar into a large bowl.

2 Put the butter or coconut oil into the bowl of a stand mixer fitted with the paddle attachment (or use an electric hand whisk), followed by the sifted dry ingredients. Beat on a low speed until it forms a fine breadcrumb texture.

3 Add a tablespoon of water and the zest (if using) and mix on a low speed. It should begin to form clumps. Continue to bring together by hand until you have one ball of dough.

4 Roll out your pastry on a lightly floured surface to a thickness of about 3mm (⅛in) for mini or small tarts and slightly thicker for one large tart/pie. If making one large tart/pie, try to roll the pastry in a neat circular shape.

5 For mini or small tarts, use a cutter slightly bigger than your tins to stamp circles of pastry, then press the pastry into the tins. For one large tart/pie, simply roll half the pastry over the rolling pin to lift, then drape over your tart tin. Press the pastry into the tin, ensuring there are no gaps. Use a sharp knife to trim any excess pastry from your tin(s) and create a neat edge. Cover the tin(s) with clingfilm (plastic wrap), then chill in the freezer for at least 3 hours, preferably overnight.

6 When ready to bake, preheat the oven to 180°C/350°F/Gas 4. For blind baking mini and small tarts I use cupcake cases to line the pastry then fill with baking beans (or uncooked rice or lentils). For a large tart/pie, cut a big piece of parchment paper, scrunch into a ball, then unravel, line the tart shell and fill with baking beans. Bake the pastry for 12–15 minutes then remove the baking beans. You can stop here if you're going to be filling and returning to the oven.

7 Bake for a further 5–10 minutes to cook through, until lightly golden (small tart cases will take less time than a large one). Leave to cool in the tins for 15 minutes before removing and transferring to a wire rack.

STOCKISTS

BAKING EQUIPMENT & DECORATING SUPPLIES

PARTY PARTY
I'd recommend a visit to this shop if you're in London but they also have an online shop. They sell cake boards, tins, decorations – pretty much everything you'll need to decorate any cake.
ppshop.co.uk

HOME CHOCOLATE FACTORY
Sells a great rage of silicone moulds for baking.
homechocolatefactory.com

LAKELAND
Sells loads of baking equipment including nozzles and piping bags. Also great for some specialist ingredients.
lakeland.co.uk

SQUIRES KITCHEN SHOP
Stocks a great range of moulds, perfect for the lollipops on page 136.
squires-shop.com

WILTON
wilton.com

N.Y. CAKE
nycake.com

SWEET CITY USA
sweetcityusa.com

INGREDIENTS

FREE FROM THAT
Specializes in ingredients for vegan and plant-based cooking, including potato protein. The price may seem expensive but it actually works out much cheaper than the price it would be per egg white.
freefromthat.com

SOUS CHEF
Sells an amazing range of specialist ingredients.
souschef.co.uk

WHOLE FOODS
wholefoodsmarket.co.uk
wholefoodsmarket.com

INDEX

A thank you to everyone who made this happen. Harriet Webster my editor for asking me to make this book and everyone else at Quadrille, including Katherine Keeble who did an amazing job of designing the book. To the dream team who created the visuals: Stephanie Claire Mcleod for the beautiful photography, Olivia Bennett for the dreamy sets and props. Both my kitchen buddies Jess Meyer and Octavia Squire for making everything run smoothly during the shoot and thank you to my good friend and make up artist, Carly Hart, for taking the day off work to come and paint everyone's arms in pastel colours. Thanks to my mum and dad for letting me wreak havoc in their kitchen for two months while I wrote this book, while I couldn't afford my London rent. Also thanks to the rest of my family and friends for being my recipe testers and eating far more sugar on the daily than one should.

Publishing Director Sarah Lavelle
Editor Harriet Webster
Designer Katherine Keeble
Photographer Stephanie McLeod
Food Stylist Sarah Hardy
Prop Stylist Olivia Bennett
Head of Production Stephen Lang
Production Controller Katie Jarvis

Published in 2020 by Quadrille,
an imprint of Hardie Grant Publishing

Quadrille
52–54 Southwark Street
London SE1 1UN
quadrille.com

Cataloguing in Publication Data: a catalogue record for
this book is available from the British Library.

ISBN 978 1 78713 519 2
Printed in China

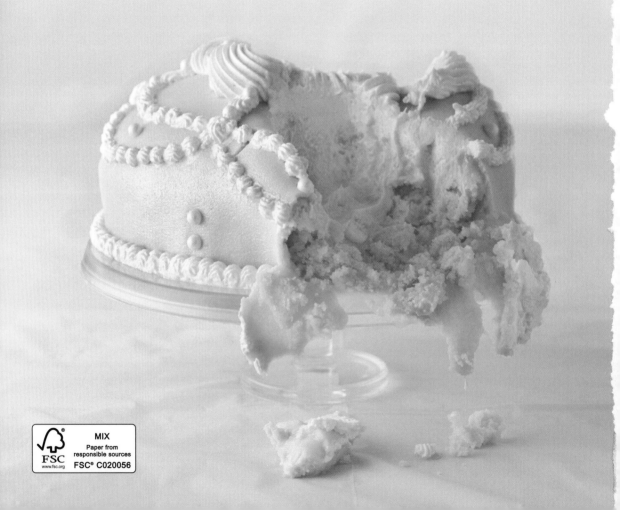